The Complete Guide to Understanding the
Holy Spirit

(Real Answers to all your Questions concerning Spiritual Gifts, Being Filled, Fruit of the Spirit, Speaking in Tongues, and more...)

WIL NICHOLS

More Than Conquer

Research Triangle Park, North Carolina

The Complete Guide to Understanding the Holy Spirit
Copyright © 2002 by Wil Nichols

Request for information should be addressed to:
More Than Conquerors Publishing
PO Box 14392, Research Triangle Park, North Carolina 27709

Library of Congress Catalog Card number: 2002107451

ISBN 0-9720999-5-6

Editors: Sharon Moore, Teresa Brooks, Grace Nichols, William Nichols Jr.

Printing in the United States of America
First Edition, 2002

Special Thanks

I want to give special thanks to the people in my life that have truly been a blessing to me!

Grace Nichols, my wife and the love of my life that has stood by me and supported me as I fulfill my assignment from God!

Anthony and Crystal Nichols, my loving children!

William and Martha Nichols Sr., my parents who raised me to be the person that I am; and who introduced me to the God of the Holy Bible!

Patrick Wooden, my father in the Lord who mentored me and taught me how to minister and serve God's people in love without compromise!

Contents

Preface

Depending on whom you talk to, you will get a wide variety of answers to the questions that many people have concerning the Holy Spirit. Each religious denomination has different opinions and teachings on the Holy Spirit. Charismatics say one thing, Baptist say another. Apostolics, Pentecostals, Methodists, and Catholics all have differing opinions concerning the Holy Spirit. Even churches within the same denomination will have views that differ.

"How do I get the Holy Spirit? How do I know when I have the Holy Spirit? Why is it taking me so long to get the Holy Spirit? Do I need the Holy Spirit? Is speaking in tongues evidence of the Holy Spirit? Why can't I speak in tongues? Why do some people speak in tongues but show no love? Why do some people show signs of the Holy Spirit but continue to sin?" You will probably get a different answer to each of these questions depending upon which denomination or church you ask.

The problem with all the differing opinions concerning the Holy Spirit is that it is hurting the body of Christ, and is totally confusing to non-believers. Some Christians may become judgmental towards other Christians. And others may feel inadequate because they think they don't have the Holy Spirit. There are even entire Christian denominations that believe that other Christian denominations are not "really saved" (true Christians) because of their practices concerning the Holy Spirit.

I personally recall an experience when my wife and I first founded the Victorious Praise Fellowship Church. We were in a small building with a sign out front that read "Church of God in Christ". As we were inside working, a young man came into the church and started witnessing to us. Apparently he had an opinion concerning our denomination and wanted to get us "really saved"! Based on the part of town we were in, this gentleman had to have walked past alcoholics, drug addicts, and prostitutes to get to us. So you see, these differing opinions concerning the Holy Spirit can prevent us from doing what we are really called to do; and that is win the lost!

Luke 4:18

18 The Spirit of the Lord is upon me, because he hath anointed me to preach the gospel to the poor; he hath sent me to heal the brokenhearted, to preach deliverance to the captives, and recovering of sight to the blind, to set at liberty them that are bruised, 1

The mission of Jesus was to preach to the poor, heal the brokenhearted, deliver the captives, recover the blind, and set the bruised free. This is also the mission of every Christian. However, if we are preoccupied with whether or not others or we have the Holy Spirit, then we are not focusing on our true purpose.

Now before you criticize this book or anything it says, please read it in its entirety. I recognize that I will be dealing with controversial issues, but I'm willing to take the heat of the controversy if you are willing to read the book. This book will biblically deal with every issue and scripture concerning the Holy Spirit, spiritual gifts, speaking in tongues, being filled with the Holy Spirit, and more.

As a pastor, I've run across many Christians who have posed questions to me concerning the Holy Spirit. I have discovered that the answers are not and should not be based

---

1 *The King James Version*, (Cambridge: Cambridge) 1769.

upon which denomination we are a part of, or what church we belong to, but should be based on a clear understanding of the purpose of the Holy Spirit as revealed in the Word of God. This book was written to answer the many questions that the Body of Christ has concerning the Holy Spirit, and prayerfully become the complete guide to understanding the Holy Spirit.

Part 1 • Real Answers to Tough Questions

Purpose

There are many people that have questions concerning the Holy Spirit. These people are Christians, non-Christians, and those seeking to know more about God. Some have become frustrated, judgmental, hypocritical, or even given up because they have not had their questions answered concerning the Holy Spirit.

1 Peter 3:15

15 Instead, you must worship Christ as Lord of your life. And if you are asked about your Christian hope, always be ready to explain it. 2

The Holy Bible says we should be ready to explain our Christian hope, our faith, and our beliefs. We need to be able to answer questions such as: Who is the Holy Spirit? What is the difference between the Holy Spirit and the Holy Ghost? How does the Holy Bible describe the Holy Spirit? What is the role of the Holy Spirit? What are the characteristics of the Holy Spirit? What is the purpose of the gifts of the Spirit? What is the purpose of the fruit of the Spirit? What if I don't have a spiritual gift? What if someone insists that I should have a particular spiritual gift? Can I choose my gift? Can my spiritual gifts become ineffective? Is one gift more important than another? Can the Holy Spirit be hindered? When do you receive the Holy Spirit? When do you lose the Holy Spirit? Can you be a Christian without the Holy Spirit? Is speaking in tongues the evidence of having the Holy Spirit? When do you become baptized or filled with the Holy Spirit? Why is blaspheming the Holy Spirit the unpardonable sin?

2*Holy Bible, New Living Translation*, (Wheaton, IL: Tyndale House Publishers, Inc.) 1996.

11

Before we begin to answer the many questions concerning the Holy Spirit, we must first understand the purpose of the Holy Spirit. If we don't understand the purpose, then any answers we obtain will be unfounded and possibly invalid. For example, if you think that the purpose of a hammer is to kill flies, then any knowledge you develop concerning the use of the hammer will be wrong. It's not that you can't kill flies with a hammer, but that is not its true purpose. Not only will the wrong purpose make you ineffective in killing flies, you may hurt someone as well. Imagine if someone has a fly on top of his or her head and you pull out your "hammer fly swatter"; someone is going to get hurt. This is what happens to the Body of Christ when we have the wrong purpose concerning the Holy Spirit.

Many Christians and non-Christians have been hurt because of not knowing the true purpose of the Holy Spirit. For example, some people place an emphasis on the demonstration of the gifts of the Holy Spirit (generally, speaking in tongues) as proof of salvation or evidence of being filled with the Holy Spirit. They will spend weeks, months, or even years trying to speak in tongues in order to convince themselves or others that they have been filled with the Holy Spirit. This emphasis on speaking in tongues has caused many to become confused or frustrated because they didn't speak in tongues. It has caused others to become insincere or hypocritical by pretending to speak in tongues. Some have even given up their salvation altogether, and all just because they couldn't pass someone's litmus test of speaking in tongues. However, the Holy Bible makes no such claim or declaration, and has never placed this type of litmus test on any Christian. Although some Christians in the Holy Bible did demonstrate the filling of the Holy Spirit through speaking in tongues, the Holy Bible has never indicated that all of us would or should do the same, and has actually indicated the opposite. We will deal with this point at great lengths later in the book, but for now lets understand the true purpose of the Holy Spirit.

The true purpose of the Holy Spirit can be revealed from his name. And yes I did say his name. The Holy Spirit is a person, not a thing. Notice the use of the pronoun "He" in the following scriptures.

John 14:26

26 But the Comforter, which is the Holy Ghost, whom the Father will send in my name, he shall teach you all things, and bring all things to your remembrance. whatsoever I have said unto you. 3

John 15:26

26 But when the Comforter is come, whom I will send unto you from the Father, even the Spirit of truth, which proceedeth from the Father, he shall testify of me: 4

Now when we look at his name (Holy Spirit), we see his purpose revealed. That purpose is to control us by moving us from a sinner to becoming like Christ. The word Holy means to be set apart, separated, or sanctified. The word Spirit means wind or breath. Wind is invisible but you see the effects of it. It is also powerful and causes movement and changes. So then the Holy Spirit is the invisible power of the Godhead that separates (sanctifies) us from the world of sin, and moves us to Christ so that we become like him. God requires us to be sanctified, holy, set apart. He then gives us the Holy Spirit to enable us to make that happen. Study the following scriptures:

---

3 *The King James Version*, (Cambridge: Cambridge) 1769.
4 *The King James Version*, (Cambridge: Cambridge) 1769.

Leviticus 20:7

7 Sanctify yourselves therefore, and be ye holy: for I am the LORD your God. 5

1 Corinthians 2:12

12 But God has given us his Spirit. That's why we don't think the same way that the people of this world think. That's also why we can recognize the blessings that God has given us. 6

2 Thessalonians 2:13

13 My friends, the Lord loves you, and it is only natural for us to thank God for you. God chose you to be the first ones to be saved. His Spirit made you holy, and you put your faith in the truth. 7

Do you see the purpose of the Holy Spirit in these scriptures? God said be Holy (set apart, separated, sanctified), and then sent the Holy Spirit to help us and move us toward Christ. This is what is known as sanctification or becoming sanctified. When you recognize that sanctification is a process and not an event, you can develop a better understanding of the purpose of the Holy Spirit, and then begin to answer some of the many questions concerning him. A person doesn't just get sanctified; he or she is in a constant perpetual state or

---

5*The King James Version*, (Cambridge: Cambridge) 1769.
6*The Contemporary English [computer file]*, electronic ed., *Logos Library System*, (Nashville: Thomas Nelson) 1997, c1995 by the American Bible Society.
7*The Contemporary English [computer file]*, electronic ed., *Logos Library System*, (Nashville: Thomas Nelson) 1997, c1995 by the American Bible Society.

process of sanctification. It is the purpose of the Holy Spirit to help us in this process.

Romans 12:1-2

1 And so, dear brothers and sisters, I plead with you to give your bodies to God. Let them be a living and holy sacrifice—the kind he will accept. When you think of what he has done for you, is this too much to ask? 2 Don't copy the behavior and customs of this world, but let God transform you into a new person by changing the way you think. Then you will know what God wants you to do, and you will know how good and pleasing and perfect his will really is. 8

Notice here that Romans 12:1 says that we are to be a holy sacrifice. Then notice that verse 2 of this chapter says it happens through God transforming us by changing the way we think. This is an ongoing continuous process that is occurring in our lives every day, every moment. It is then the Holy Spirit that is helping us to transform our minds.

John 14:26

26 But the Holy Spirit will come and help you, because the Father will send the Spirit to take my place. The Spirit will teach you everything and will remind you of what I said while I was with you. 9

Let me restate the purpose of the Holy Spirit. **The purpose of the Holy Spirit is to separate (sanctify) us from the world of sin, and move us toward Christ so that we**

8*Holy Bible, New Living Translation*, (Wheaton, IL: Tyndale House Publishers, Inc.) 1996.
9*The Contemporary English [computer file], electronic ed., Logos Library System*, (Nashville: Thomas Nelson) 1997, c1995 by the American Bible Society.

become like him. Now when you look at the purpose of Jesus Christ, you can then see how the purpose of the Holy Spirit works in concert with Christ's purpose.

If you recall, Jesus revealed his purpose in Luke 4:18 when he said he was anointed to preach to the poor, heal the brokenhearted, deliver the captives, recover the blind, and set the bruised free. The Holy Spirit moves us to become like Christ so that we can take on his same purpose.

Matthew 28:18-20

18 Jesus came to them and said: I have been given all authority in heaven and on earth! 19 Go to the people of all nations and make them my disciples. Baptize them in the name of the Father, the Son, and the Holy Spirit, 20 and teach them to do everything I have told you. I will be with you always, even until the end of the world. 10

John 16:7-8

7 But I tell you that I am going to do what is best for you. That is why I am going away. The Holy Spirit cannot come to help you until I leave. But after I am gone, I will send the Spirit to you. 8 The Spirit will come and show the people of this world the truth about sin and God's justice and the judgment. 11

Jesus was saying in these scriptures, go and make my mission your mission; and I will send the Holy Spirit to help you accomplish it. **The purpose of the Holy Spirit is not to**

10*The Contemporary English [computer file], electronic ed., Logos Library System*, (Nashville: Thomas Nelson) 1997, c1995 by the American Bible Society.
11*The Contemporary English [computer file], electronic ed., Logos Library System*, (Nashville: Thomas Nelson) 1997, c1995 by the American Bible Society.

prove salvation, it is not to make us speak in tongues, it is not to make us deep, it is not to make us dance or shout, but it is to make us more like Christ so that we can carry out his mission of winning the world. Any Christian preoccupied with any other purpose, is not accomplishing what we were called to do.

Before I close this chapter out, I want to make one more point about purpose. Note that Jesus himself gave us most of the scriptures that reveal the purpose of the Holy Spirit. He was generally speaking to his disciples explaining to them this person called the Holy Spirit, who would come and take his place when he left. Now since Jesus is part of the Godhead, then I think he should be the authority on the purpose of the Holy Spirit. The Holy Spirit may cause us to dance and shout, it may cause us to demonstrate spiritual gifts such as speaking in tongues, but Jesus never said these things were the purpose of the Holy Spirit. We will learn more about purpose as we study the fruit and gifts of the Holy Spirit in subsequent chapters.

How Does The Holy Spirit Work?

God is tri-part, made up of God the Father, God the Son, and God the Holy Spirit. He created us in his image, and thus made us tri-part: body, soul, and spirit. Our souls are also tri-part, made up of our mind, our will, and our emotions. Our soul then is what we think (mind), what we do (will), and what we feel (emotions). It is the spirit that controls the soul; controlling what we think, do, and feel. When we are born, the spirit that is controlling the soul is the human or sinful spirit.

Psalm 51:5

5 Behold, I was shapen in iniquity; and in sin did my mother conceive me. 12

From birth, our human spirit controls what we think, what we do, and what we feel. Perhaps you have made or have heard others make the following statements: "I don't know why I'm thinking this way!" " I don't know why I did that!" "I don't know why I still love him!" The reason for these statements is that the human spirit is in control of the soul. How do we change this? By taking the control of the soul from the human spirit, and giving it to the Holy Spirit. (See Figures 1 & 2)

12*The King James Version*, (Cambridge: Cambridge) 1769.

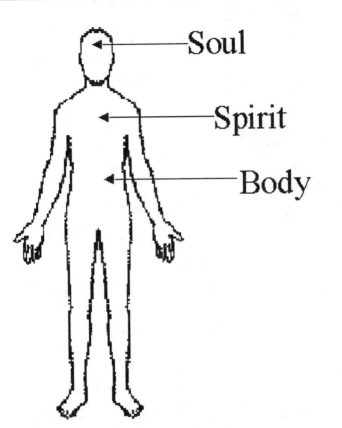

Figure 1: Just as God is tri-part,
Consisting of God the Father, God
the Son, and God the Holy Spirit; So
are we tri-part, made up of Body,
Soul, and Spirit!

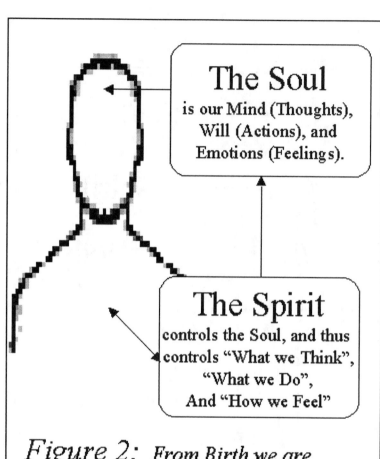

The Soul
is our Mind (Thoughts),
Will (Actions), and
Emotions (Feelings).

The Spirit
controls the Soul, and thus
controls "What we Think",
"What we Do",
And "How we Feel"

Figure 2: *From Birth we are controlled by the Human or Worldly Spirit. When we accept Christ, the Holy Spirit takes over the control of the Soul! This is what it means to "Walk in the Spirit"*

When we accept the Holy Spirit into our heart, he replaces the role of the human or sinful spirit in us. And when this happens, our soul comes under new management. The Holy Spirit is now controlling the soul. He is teaching us what to think, directing us in what to do, and controlling us with regards to our emotions. This is what is known as "Walking in the Spirit". Study the following scriptures:

Galatians 5:16

16 This I say then, Walk in the Spirit, and ye shall not fulfil the lust of the flesh. 13

Romans 8:1-2

1 So now there is no condemnation for those who belong to Christ Jesus. 2 For the power of the life-giving Spirit has freed you through Christ Jesus from the power of sin that leads to death. 14

Psalm 119:11

11 Thy word have I hid in mine heart, that I might not sin against thee.

2 Corinthians 10:4-5

4 (For the weapons of our warfare are not carnal, but mighty through God to the pulling down of strong holds;) 5 Casting down imaginations, and every high thing that exalteth itself against the knowledge of God, and bringing into captivity every thought to the obedience of Christ; 15

13*The King James Version*, (Cambridge: Cambridge) 1769.
14*Holy Bible, New Living Translation*, (Wheaton, IL: Tyndale House Publishers, Inc.) 1996.
15*The King James Version*, (Cambridge: Cambridge) 1769.

Perhaps you have heard of a young lady that has been in love with a man that was simply no good. Everyone could see that this guy was trouble except her. And sometimes even after his character was revealed to her, she would stay with him because her emotions told her she was in love with him. I have seen young ladies go as far as give up their relationship with God to follow after a non-Christian man. Clearly the Holy Spirit is not in control of the emotions in these cases.

Maybe you have heard someone say, "I don't know why I did that!" Well I do! It's because the Holy Bible says, as a man thinks then so is he. So if the Word of God is not feeding his thoughts, then the Holy Spirit is not directing his will (behavior).

Instead of thinking what our sinful nature wants us to think, we need to think the thoughts that the Holy Spirit wants us to think.

Romans 8:27

27 And he that searcheth the hearts knoweth what is the mind of the Spirit, because he maketh intercession for the saints according to the will of God. 16

Instead of doing our will, we need to do the will of the Holy Spirit:

1 Corinthians 12:11

11 But all these worketh that one and the selfsame Spirit, dividing to every man severally as he will. 17

16*The King James Version*, (Cambridge: Cambridge) 1769.
17*The King James Version*, (Cambridge: Cambridge) 1769.

Instead of being led by our emotions, we need the emotions of the Holy Spirit:

Romans 15:30

30 Now I beseech you, brethren, for the Lord Jesus Christ's sake, and for the love of the Spirit, that ye strive together with me in your prayers to God for me; 18

If we are ever going to totally walk in God's purpose, we are going to have to allow the Holy Spirit to control our soul (thoughts, will, and emotions). We will then be thinking the right thoughts, doing the right things, and feeling the right emotions.

18*The King James Version*, (Cambridge: Cambridge) 1769.

The Introduction of the Holy Spirit

We've touched on the role of the Holy Spirit in the chapter titled "Purpose", but let's look at it a little more in depth. We will start by looking at the fulfilling of the promise of the Holy Spirit in the second chapter of Acts.

Acts 2:1-4

And when the day of Pentecost was fully come, they were all with one accord in one place. 2 And suddenly there came a sound from heaven as of a rushing mighty wind, and it filled all the house where they were sitting. 3 And there appeared unto them cloven tongues like as of fire, and it sat upon each of them. 4 And they were all filled with the Holy Ghost, and began to speak with other tongues, as the Spirit gave them utterance. 19

A lot of people point to this scripture as instructions on how to be filled with the Holy Spirit. They will say that since the people in this passage of scripture were filled with the Holy Spirit and all of them spoke in tongues, then this is the way we should be filled with the Holy Spirit. But there are two problems with this assumption. The first problem is simply with the improper interpretation of this passage of scripture as "instructional". There is nothing in this passage that would indicate that it is instructional. There are no words such as "do this', "don't do that", "Thou shall", "Thou shall not". Whenever God wanted to instruct us in the Holy Bible, he would always be very clear. He would say things like "Thou shall not have other gods before me", "Thou shall not kill", "Walk in the Spirit", or "Be not conformed to this

---

19*The King James Version*, (Cambridge: Cambridge) 1769.

world". These are instructions. The passage below is an example of a passage that is NOT instructional.

Exodus 14:21-22

21 Moses stretched his arm over the sea, and the LORD sent a strong east wind that blew all night until there was dry land where the water had been. The sea opened up, 22 and the Israelites walked through on dry land with a wall of water on each side. 20

This is not telling us as Christians that we have the ability to part the seas. You can jump into a lake with a stick in our hands if you want, but if God didn't tell you to do it, then the next time I see you will probably be in heaven. Although I'm being somewhat comical here, I'm trying to show you the point that all scripture is not instructional. Some scripture is merely the telling of an event that occurred. Yes it still benefits us, but it is not telling us to do the same thing. And so it is with the second chapter of Acts. There is a beneficial reason why this passage of scripture was placed in the Holy Bible, but proper interpretation will show you that it's not instructional.

Let us first look at the timeframe of the passage. The timeframe is not a coincidence, as you will see.

Acts 2:1

And when the day of Pentecost was fully come, they were all with one accord in one place. 21

20*The Contemporary English [computer file], electronic ed., Logos Library System,* (Nashville: Thomas Nelson) 1997, c1995 by the American Bible Society.
21*The King James Version,* (Cambridge: Cambridge) 1769.

This chapter starts out by giving us a timeframe. It was a specific day, the day of Pentecost. Pentecost was the third great Israeli feast mentioned in Leviticus 23. It was a harvest festival celebrated fifty days after the Passover week. Jews from all over, even from foreign countries, would come together for this celebration. Now if we are to use Acts 2 as instruction for every Christian, then we should use the timeframe as instruction as well. So then step one of our instruction would be that you could only be filled on the celebration day of Pentecost.

Acts 2:2-3

2 And suddenly there came a sound from heaven as of a rushing mighty wind, and it filled all the house where they were sitting. 3 And there appeared unto them cloven tongues like as of fire, and it sat upon each of them. 22

Now again, if this passage was instructional, then all these events should also occur. The Holy Bible was not being metaphoric here, these events did occur. And if it's instructional, then it should occur the same way for all of us today. So we should hear a loud sound of wind (I would image something like a tornado), which should fill whatever house we are in. There should also be tongues that look like fire, that we can see, that eventually settles on each of us. Again the Holy Bible is being very literal here. It says that the tongues of fire appeared unto them. Now I don't know about you, but I've been in some powerful spirit filled services, but I've never heard a rushing wind, and I've never seen tongues of fire.

Acts 2:4

22*The King James Version*, (Cambridge: Cambridge) 1769.

4 And they were all filled with the Holy Ghost, and began to speak with other tongues, as the Spirit gave them utterance. 23

Many Christians will take this one verse and say it's instructional, and therefore the only way to be filled with the Holy Spirit is to speak in tongues as these individuals did here in verse four. But what about the first three verses. If verse four is to happen to every Christian this exact way, then so should verses one through three. But let us continue studying this passage!

Acts 2:5-8

5 Now there were staying in Jerusalem God-fearing Jews from every nation under heaven. 6 When they heard this sound, a crowd came together in bewilderment, because each one heard them speaking in his own language. 7 Utterly amazed, they asked: "Are not all these men who are speaking Galileans? 8 Then how is it that each of us hears them in his own native language? 24

Again, if the second chapter of Acts is the instructions for Christians on what should happen when they receive the Holy Spirit; then according to verses five through eight of this chapter, whenever we are filled with the Holy Spirit, there must also be men from foreign countries there as witnesses that we are speaking in their languages.

From an instructional standpoint, there are a lot of events that have to happen in order for us to be filled with the Holy Spirit if we are to use the second chapter of Acts as our instructions. But if we interpret this passage of scripture

---

23*The King James Version*, (Cambridge: Cambridge) 1769.
24*The New International Version*, (Grand Rapids, MI: Zondervan Publishing House) 1984.

properly, we will see its true purpose. Let's look at a few verses later in the chapter.

Acts 2:12-16

12 Amazed and perplexed, they asked one another, "What does this mean?" 13 Some, however, made fun of them and said, "They have had too much wine." 14 Then Peter stood up with the Eleven, raised his voice and addressed the crowd: "Fellow Jews and all of you who live in Jerusalem, let me explain this to you; listen carefully to what I say. 15 These men are not drunk, as you suppose. It's only nine in the morning! 16 No, this is what was spoken by the prophet Joel: 25

Proper interpretation of this passage reveals that this event (the coming of the Holy Spirit in the form and role that we know him today), was prophesied in Joel 2:28, and that everything that happened was for a specific purpose. Up to this point, the Holy Spirit had not dealt with man this way. Something new was being introduced to man. Let's answer a few questions to get proper understanding of what was going on here.

What is the significance of the Day of Pentecost? Why were there foreigners at this event? When you properly study the second chapter of Acts, you recognize that the answers to these two questions are connected to each other. The foreigners that were at this event were there because of the Pentecost celebration. I've heard people improperly interpret Acts 2:1 to mean that the Holy Spirit will only come when we are all on one accord (*Acts 2:1 And when the day of Pentecost was fully come, they were all with one accord in one place).* The Holy Spirit didn't come because they were on one accord;

25*The New International Version*, (Grand Rapids, MI: Zondervan Publishing House) 1984.

it came because it was the day of Pentecost. The Pentecost celebration was the event that caused the foreigners to come to town. The Holy Spirit wouldn't come until these foreigners were in place so that they could be the witnesses of the miraculous event. When these foreigners heard these men speaking in their languages (which was a miracle), it allowed them to be the first witnesses of the coming of the Holy Spirit in this new form. It gave Peter the opportunity to preach to them about the prophesy of the Prophet Joel, and it became the catalyst for the formation of the first Christian church.

What was the purpose of the "rushing mighty wind and the cloven tongues like fire"? Now this is merely conjecture on my part, but if you stick with this being an event to introduce the Holy Spirit in it's new form to man; then the purpose of the rushing mighty wind can be compared to the pomp and circumstance that would occur when a new King was introduced. In times past, trumpets or horns would be blown to signal the entrance of a King. Well, I liken the rushing mighty wind to God's ceremonial introduction of the Holy Spirit to us. Now again this is conjecture, so don't take it as Gospel. But if you stay with this train of thought, it would explain why we never see this in the Holy Bible again. The point being that once the Holy Spirit is introduced, there would be no reason to introduce him again.

Why did all the men speak in tongues? Well first of all they did not speak in unknown tongues, as many Christians do today (we will study unknown tongues in a later chapter), but they spoke in foreign languages. Now remember that the foreigners were there because of the Pentecost celebration. I believe that God orchestrated this entire series of events for the expressed purpose of introducing the Holy Spirit to man. He chose this day, brought the witnesses together, blew his trumpet, and then filled everyone with the Holy Spirit. He then chose the miracle of having everyone speak in a foreign language to be the key event of the introduction. Now although the purpose I gave for the rushing wind and tongues of fires were conjecture on my part, everything else I've stated here in this chapter falls in line with proper contextual and historical scripture interpretation.

The Role of the Holy Spirit

When we look at the Holy Spirit, we recognize him as a person who is part of a team. The team that I'm referring to is the Godhead: God the Father, God the Son, and God the Holy Spirit. We know that they are a team because we see them working together in Genesis.

Genesis 1:26

26 And God said, Let us make man in our image, after our likeness: and let them have dominion over the fish of the sea, and over the fowl of the air, and over the cattle, and over all the earth, and over every creeping thing that creepeth upon the earth. 26

Here we see God assembling the team to make man because he says here "Let us make man". When I worked at IBM as a computer programmer and later as a manager, I learned the value of teamwork. We had to create computer programs that had thousands upon thousands of computer instructions. In the short timeframe in which we had to develop the programs, one man couldn't do it all by himself. We had to get many people to work together. And although we worked together, we all couldn't do the same thing at the same time. In order for us to be successful, we had to give each member of the team his or her separate role. When everyone did his or her role successfully, the computer program was completed on time. Just like I had a role to perform on my team, the Holy Spirit has a role to perform on his team.

26*The King James Version*, (Cambridge: Cambridge) 1769.

The Holy Spirit before Acts 2

Although the Holy Spirit is introduced to man in the form that we know him today, he has always existed. And like any other person, he has had many roles.

To celebrate the sixtieth birthday of my father, I was asked to wear a tuxedo and make a formal presentation at a prestigious banquet that was being held in his honor. If that was the first time you saw me, you could have developed an opinion about me that would have been incorrect. You may have thought that I was a very formal, stoic, conservative person. You would have incorrectly developed an opinion about me based on seeing me in only one role. But I serve in many roles. I'm a pastor, husband, father, entrepreneur, teacher, musician, and more. Well the Holy Spirit is a person that serves in more than the role we see him performing in the second chapter of Acts. He's more than just the person that caused a group of men to speak in tongues. If you think of the Holy Spirit as just a spirit to make you speak in tongues, then you have a very narrow view of who he is.

If you want to know who Pastor Wil is, don't just evaluate me on how I was last Monday. It's only one day! It may have been a good day, or it may have been a bad day. If you base your whole opinion of me on one encounter, then you are being narrow-minded. You need to be more open-minded than that. Now don't misunderstand me, there is a time to be narrow minded. For example, if you are planning a party for your African-American friend that is really into his culture, you might want to leave out the square dancing and country line dancing with Slim Whitman music. Likewise, there are times we should be narrow-minded when it comes to the Holy Spirit. For example, if a spirit comes to you telling you to go and sleep with your married friend's spouse, you might not want to be open-minded at that time.

That being said, let's open our mind a little to get to know the whole person of the Holy Spirit, by studying his many roles in the Holy Bible.

First of all he assisted with the creation of the earth.

Genesis 1:1-2

In the beginning God created the heaven and the earth. 2 And the earth was without form, and void; and darkness was upon the face of the deep. And the Spirit of God moved upon the face of the waters. 27

The earth is described as being without form, void, and in darkness.   This would indicate the absence of God. "Without form" is the Hebrew word tohu, meaning ruin or vacancy.   "Void" is the Hebrew word bohu, meaning emptiness.

The next verse then says the Spirit of God moved upon the face of the waters. The word for "moved" in the Hebrew means brooded, like a mother hen broods over her little chicks. He brooded upon the face of the waters. The Holy Spirit began a ministry here, which we will find Him doing again and again throughout the Holy Bible. It is the ministry of preparation.

John 3:5

5 Jesus answered, Verily, verily, I say unto thee, Except a man be born of water and of the Spirit, he cannot enter into the kingdom of God. 28

27*The King James Version*, (Cambridge: Cambridge) 1769.
28*The King James Version*, (Cambridge: Cambridge) 1769.

Now we know that the Spirit here is the Holy Spirit, but what is the water? Some will say baptism, and that's fine, but to be baptized in water is only symbolic. If you are an unrepentant sinner, water baptism will do you no good. I have a saying, "You will go under the water a dry sinner, and come out of the water a wet sinner". So what does it really mean to be born of water and of the Spirit? Water is symbolic of cleansing, and the thing that really cleanses us is the Word of God.

John 17:17

17 Sanctify them through thy truth: thy word is truth.29

There is a cleansing, sanctifying power in the Word of God.

John 15:3

3 Now ye are clean through the word which I have spoken unto you. 30

The Word of God is likened unto water again and again. Jesus says in John 3:5 that man needs water (the Word), and the Spirit to be reborn. Now in Genesis, before God uses the Word to create the earth, the Spirit of God moves upon it. So if we look at man in the same way, we can conclude that before the Word can cause rebirth in a man, the Spirit of God has to move upon him. Just as the Spirit of God prepared the earth to receive the Word of God, it also prepares us to receive his Word. As a matter of fact, the Word cannot change us until the Spirit moves upon us to receive it. If the Spirit of God didn't move upon us when we were sinners, then we would have never accepted the Word of God and repented

---

29*The King James Version*, (Cambridge: Cambridge) 1769.
30*The King James Version*, (Cambridge: Cambridge) 1769.

of our sins. The role of the Holy Spirit here then is a ministry of preparation.

As a pastor, I can teach and preach until I'm blue in the face; but it's not until the Holy Spirit moves upon the heart of a man, that you will see a tough rough-neck man with tears in his eyes give his heart to the Lord.

This role of the Holy Spirit existed well before the second chapter of Acts. But there are other roles of the Holy Spirit we see in operation at various times in the Holy Bible. Sometimes the Holy Spirit would come upon men and bestow supernatural abilities.

In Genesis 41:38, the Spirit bestowed supernatural wisdom in Joseph to interpret Pharaoh's dream concerning the coming famine.

In Numbers 27:18, the Spirit came upon Joshua to give him the strength to be the successor to Moses.

In 1 Samuel 16:14, the Spirit of the Lord left King Saul because of his deliberate disobedience.

The Holy Spirit caused men to prophesy (2 Peter 1:21), and he caused the conception of Jesus in Mary (Luke 1:35).

The Holy Spirit after Acts 2

The role of the Holy Spirit after the second chapter of Acts is basically a role of abiding in us to bring about change from a sinful nature to a life that is like Christ. This causes us to fulfill the purpose of Christ. Think about the Holy Spirit as the batteries to a flashlight. The flashlight cannot work to produce light until batteries are placed within it. And so it is with the Holy Spirit.

Matthew 5:14

14 Ye are the light of the world. A city that is set on an hill cannot be hid. 31

The Holy Spirit produces light that directs us towards God's purpose.

The 7 Roles of the Holy Spirit

Another analogy that I like concerning the role of the Holy Spirit is that of a coach. When I first moved to North Carolina, I met a powerful man named Pastor Patrick Wooden. He was a powerful Spirit-led Pastor, filled with the Holy Spirit. But he was also physically powerful as a body builder who constantly worked out at the gym. As our friendship grew, he invited me to the gym to workout. When I first started working out, I could barely bench-press 135 pounds. After one year of working out with him, I was bench-pressing over 300 pounds. My Pastor and spiritual leader became my coach and physical leader.

My Pastor coached me four days a week, 6:00 am in the morning, every week for an entire year. He taught me how to workout, how to build my strength, and how to regenerate my body. He encouraged and motivated me to continue to workout. He communicated with me on a regular basis and we became great friends. But he never lifted one weight for me, he never pulled me out of the bed in the morning, and he never ran one mile for me. His role was to coach (lead, guide, teach); my role was to do what he said.

---

31 *The King James Version*, (Cambridge: Cambridge) 1769.

The Holy Spirit is our coach. If we learn from him and do what he says, we will become more like Christ and walk in the will and purpose of God.

John 14:26

26 But the Comforter, which is the Holy Ghost, whom the Father will send in my name, he shall teach you all things, and bring all things to your remembrance, whatsoever I have said unto you. 32

John 16:7-8

7 But it is actually best for you that I go away, because if I don't, the Counselor won't come. If I do go away, he will come because I will send him to you. 8 And when he comes, he will convince the world of its sin, and of God's righteousness, and of the coming judgment. 33

Here are seven roles of the Holy Spirit that assist the Christian believer in performing God's purpose.

1. Conviction: *John 16:8 And when he comes, he will convince the world of its sin, and of God's righteousness, and of the coming judgment. 34*

2. Regeneration: *Titus 3:5 Not by works of righteousness which we have done, but according to his mercy he saved us, by the washing of regeneration, and renewing of the Holy Ghost; 35*

32*The King James Version*, (Cambridge: Cambridge) 1769.
33*Holy Bible, New Living Translation*, (Wheaton, IL: Tyndale House Publishers, Inc.) 1996.
34*Holy Bible, New Living Translation*, (Wheaton, IL: Tyndale House Publishers, Inc.) 1996.
35*The King James Version*, (Cambridge: Cambridge) 1769.

3. Connection: *1 Corinthians 12:13 For by one Spirit are we all baptized into one body, whether we be Jews or Gentiles, whether we be bond or free; and have been all made to drink into one Spirit. 36*

4. Sealing: *2 Corinthians 1:22 Who hath also sealed us, and given the earnest of the Spirit in our hearts. 37*

5. Indwelling: *1 Corinthians 3:16 Know ye not that ye are the temple of God, and that the Spirit of God dwelleth in you? 38*

6. Controlling: *Ephesians 5:18 And be not drunk with wine, wherein is excess; but be filled with the Spirit; 39*

7. Communication: *Romans 8:26 Likewise the Spirit also helpeth our infirmities: for we know not what we should pray for as we ought: but the Spirit itself maketh intercession for us with groanings which cannot be uttered. 40*

36*The King James Version*, (Cambridge: Cambridge) 1769.
37*The King James Version*, (Cambridge: Cambridge) 1769.
38*The King James Version*, (Cambridge: Cambridge) 1769.
39*The King James Version*, (Cambridge: Cambridge) 1769.
40*The King James Version*, (Cambridge: Cambridge) 1769.

Obstacles to the Holy Spirit

When we think of God the Holy Spirit, we may think of a being that is all-powerful, capable of doing anything. I've often heard people say that the reason people are not acting right and living right is because they don't have the Holy Ghost (Holy Spirit). My assumption is that they believe that the Holy Spirit will somehow make them live a saved and righteous life. As a pastor, I've even counseled people who believe that something is wrong with them because they have not been able to live a perfect life free from sin. They wonder why they are still tempted with evil thoughts, why sometimes they have even given in to those temptations. How can this be possible if we have the Holy Spirit? Are there really things we can do that create obstacles to the Holy Spirit? Do these obstacles prevent the Holy Spirit from performing his role in our lives?

Before we answer these questions, let's quickly review how the Holy Spirit works within our body! We are made up of the body, soul, and spirit. The soul is made up of the mind, will, and emotions, and is controlled by the spirit. However, from birth, the spirit that is controlling the soul is the human or worldly spirit. This human spirit is then determining what we think, how we act, and what we feel. But when we accept Christ, the Holy Spirit moves in to provide control (guidance) to the soul. He then teaches us what to think, directs us how to act, and provides control over our emotions.

2 Corinthians 10:3-5

3 We are human, but we don't wage war with human plans and methods. 4 We use God's mighty weapons, not mere worldly weapons, to knock down the Devil's strongholds. 5 With these weapons we break down every proud argument that keeps people from knowing God. With these weapons we conquer their rebellious ideas, and we teach them to obey Christ. 41

There is a transformation process that occurs as a result of the Holy Spirit coming into our hearts. However, there can be obstacles that can hinder this transformation process.

Romans 12:2

2 Don't copy the behavior and customs of this world, but let God transform you into a new person by changing the way you think. Then you will know what God wants you to do, and you will know how good and pleasing and perfect his will really is. 42

In the following sections, I will discuss five obstacles that get in the way of the Holy Spirit performing his role in our lives. They are 1) Ignoring the Weather Report, 2) Quenching the Holy Spirit, 3) Grieving the Holy Spirit, 4) Lack of Faith, and 5) Resisting the Holy Spirit.

Ignoring the Weather Report

The analogy I'd like to use to explain how we can hinder the Holy Spirit's ability to transform us is "Ignoring the Weather Report". A while back, a movie was released titled "The Perfect Storm". In this movie, three storms converged to create a cataclysmic phenomenon that they called a perfect storm. As a result of this storm, many lives were needlessly lost. They were lost not so much because of the storm, but

---

41*Holy Bible, New Living Translation*, (Wheaton, IL: Tyndale House Publishers, Inc.) 1996.
42*Holy Bible, New Living Translation*, (Wheaton, IL: Tyndale House Publishers, Inc.) 1996.

because the people ignored the weather report. The meteorologist had reported earlier that the storms were coming, but most of the people simply ignored his report.

Many years ago, whenever a hurricane would hit the country, hundreds and sometimes thousands of people would lose their lives. But in my lifetime, very few people have died as a result of a hurricane hitting the United States. The reason is because of the weather reports we get from the meteorologist. People hear the weather reports, and act accordingly. They move inland, move to safer ground, board up homes, and move into shelters. Lives are saved because we do not ignore the weather reports.

From a spiritual perspective, the Holy Spirit is our spiritual meteorologist. If we listen to his weather reports, we will avoid many trials of life. As Christians, we could have avoided much heartache, disappointments, bad relationships, sinful acts, and other situations if we would have only listened to our spiritual weather report. The Holy Spirit told us to hold our peace, but we just had to tell that person off. The Holy Spirit told us to not go over that person's house by ourselves, but we did it anyway. These were warnings from our meteorologist, but we ignored them. I know that I'm guilty of having ignored my weather reports in the past.

Quenching the Holy Spirit

To quench something means to extinguish, douse, smother, or suppress. As Christians we can hinder the work of the Holy Spirit in our lives by suppressing it!

Perhaps you have been on a job where you really had a lot to contribute. However your coworkers or supervisor may have felt intimidated or threatened by you. As a result, whenever you tried to contribute new ideas, they would always be shot down for one reason or another. Eventually you got to the point where you didn't want to try any more. You had just been "quenched"! Your views, ideas, contributions had been smothered or suppressed. As Christians, we can do the same thing to the Holy Spirit!

1 Thessalonians 5:19

19 Quench not the Spirit. 43

When we first accepted Christ, the Holy Spirit came rushing in ready to do his job. The Holy Spirit gave us ideas on how to become more like Christ, how to overcome sin and strongholds, and how to live a more abundant, prosperous, and blessed life. However, we may have been in a state of quenching the Holy Spirit. When the Holy Spirit told some of us to let go of certain unhealthy relationships, we may have rejected his ideas because we were in love. When he told us to tithe or give offerings in church, we may have also rejected these ideas because we couldn't afford it. When the Holy Spirit compelled us to change certain behaviors, we may have rejected those ideas as well, feeling that we were just being ourselves. By refusing to act, speak, or respond to the direction and guidance from the Holy Spirit, we are quenching or suppressing him. This in turn prevents us from truly walking in the Spirit. It makes us ineffective as Christians, and irrelevant in the completion of God's purpose. How can a general be successful if half the soldiers suppress his ideas? How can God's purpose be successful in our lives if we are quenching the Spirit?

Grieving the Holy Spirit

43*The King James Version*, (Cambridge: Cambridge) 1769.

The Holy Bible indicates that we can grieve the Holy Spirit.

Ephesians 4:30

30 And grieve not the holy Spirit of God, whereby ye are sealed unto the day of redemption. 44

To grieve means to bring sorrow, anguish, affliction, or distress as a result of one's behavior. Any parent that has had a wayward child understands what it means to be grieved. We all can perhaps identify with a mother that brings her first son into the world. She perhaps has dreams of her son having a successful life. She envisions him working as a manager of a major corporation, or maybe as an entrepreneur of his own company. But as a result of disobedience and bad decisions, she sees his life spiral downward until he ends up in prison.

As Christians, we can grieve the Holy Spirit just as a child can grieve his mother.

1 Corinthians 6:15

15 Don't you realize that your bodies are actually parts of Christ? Should a man take his body, which belongs to Christ, and join it to a prostitute? Never! 45

1 Corinthians 6:19

19 Or don't you know that your body is the temple of the Holy Spirit, who lives in you and was given to you by God? You do not belong to yourself, 46

44*The King James Version*, (Cambridge: Cambridge) 1769.

45*Holy Bible, New Living Translation*, (Wheaton, IL: Tyndale House Publishers, Inc.) 1996.

46*Holy Bible, New Living Translation*, (Wheaton, IL: Tyndale House Publishers, Inc.) 1996.

Our behavior can grieve the Holy Spirit. He's been sent here to live in us, help us become like Christ, and help us to have a successful life while here on earth. But our behavior can disrupt God's plan for our lives, and this in-turn will grieve the Holy Spirit.

Lack of Faith

All our lives we have been taught to be self-sufficient and self-reliant. "Get an education", "Go to college", "Get a good job", and "Buy a home" are all phrases that we have heard at one point or another. Now don't misunderstand me, I believe that all of these things should be done; however, they also teach us to depend upon our own abilities. And when we come to depend upon our own abilities too much, we will not depend upon God. This is what is meant by a lack of faith. Having a lack of faith creates problems for the Holy Spirit.

Hebrews 11:6

6 So, you see, it is impossible to please God without faith. Anyone who wants to come to him must believe that there is a God and that he rewards those who sincerely seek him. 47

In dealing with us, God operates in the Spirit through faith. When we lack faith, then our ability to communicate with God is inhibited. It's like talking on a cell phone with a bad connection. Both parties are talking, but you are missing half the message. When we lack faith, we miss much of what God has for us.

47*Holy Bible, New Living Translation*, (Wheaton, IL: Tyndale House Publishers, Inc.) 1996.

1 Corinthians 2:14

14 But the natural man receiveth not the things of the Spirit of God: for they are foolishness unto him: neither can he know them, because they are spiritually discerned. 48

Because it takes faith to communicate with the Spirit of God, if we are lacking faith we are not walking according to the Spirit. And if we are not walking in the Spirit, then we are walking after the flesh; that is to say we are walking according to our natural abilities. We then cannot receive the things of God because naturally they make no sense.

A few years ago before I started Victorious Praise Fellowship Church, God led me to leave a good paying job in corporate America. My experience was in computer programming, project management, and people management; and my salary was over $100,000 per year. I was living a good life, making good money, married to a beautiful woman, and had two lovely children. With things going so well, you can image what raced through my mind when God called me to Pastor, start a church, and walk off my job.

Any lack of faith on my part would have been an obstacle. There is no way I would have made this move unless I had enough faith to hear and move according to the will of God.

We can't receive the things of the Spirit if there's a lack of faith. We will think thoughts like "I just can't see it", "It won't work", "I don't have enough money", "We are moving too fast", "We don't have enough people", "We can't get there from here", or "It is just not possible"! But when we have faith, we begin to live according to the Word of God:

48*The King James Version*, (Cambridge: Cambridge) 1769.

Philippians 4:13

13 I can do all things through Christ which strengtheneth me. 49

Matthew 19:26

26 But Jesus beheld them, and said unto them, With men this is impossible; but with God all things are possible. 50

This next passage of scripture really sums up the concept of why a lack of faith is an obstacle to the Holy Spirit.

1 Corinthians 2:9-16

9 But as it is written, Eye hath not seen, nor ear heard, neither have entered into the heart of man, the things which God hath prepared for them that love him. 10 But God hath revealed them unto us by his Spirit: for the Spirit searcheth all things, yea, the deep things of God. 11 For what man knoweth the things of a man, save the spirit of man which is in him? even so the things of God knoweth no man, but the Spirit of God. 12 Now we have received, not the spirit of the world, but the spirit which is of God; that we might know the things that are freely given to us of God. 13 Which things also we speak, not in the words which man's wisdom teacheth, but which the Holy Ghost teacheth; comparing spiritual things with spiritual. 14 But the natural man receiveth not the things of the Spirit of God: for they are foolishness unto him: neither can he know them, because they are spiritually discerned. 15 But he that is spiritual judgeth all things, yet he himself is judged of no man. 16 For who hath known the mind of the Lord, that he may instruct him? But we have the mind of Christ. 51

49*The King James Version*, (Cambridge: Cambridge) 1769.
50*The King James Version*, (Cambridge: Cambridge) 1769.
51*The King James Version*, (Cambridge: Cambridge) 1769.

Paul even rebukes the church concerning a lack of faith in the following passage:

Galatians 3:1-3

1 You stupid Galatians! I told you exactly how Jesus Christ was nailed to a cross. Has someone now put an evil spell on you? 2 I want to know only one thing. How were you given God's Spirit? Was it by obeying the Law of Moses or by hearing about Christ and having faith in him? 3 How can you be so stupid? Do you think that by yourself you can complete what God's Spirit started in you? 52

Resisting the Holy Spirit

I like watching science fiction movies and television shows. One of the shows I particularly like is Star Trek. On this futuristic show, the main characters are constantly faced with various villains. One of the villains is called the Borg. They are a race of cyber-genetic creatures that take over one's body, regardless of any resistance. The first words they utter whenever they encounter potential victims is "Resistance is Futile."

Well, unfortunately, unlike the Borg, this is not how the Holy Spirit works. He does not take over your body and somehow make you live a saved, sanctified, and holy life for God. He is only there to help you if you want to live saved.

James 4:7

52*The Contemporary English [computer file], electronic ed., Logos Library System*, (Nashville: Thomas Nelson) 1997, c1995 by the American Bible Society.

7 Surrender to God! Resist the devil, and he will run from you. 53

This passage says that if you resist the Devil, he will run from you. Well if you resist the Holy Spirit, then you will have a similar result. Recalling the analogy of the Holy Spirit being like a coach who is willing to teach and train us; if we tell the coach to get lost, he will simply move on to someone who wants to be trained. Everything about the Holy Spirit and his role in our life is about choices. He will give us power over any sin, he will teach and train us, he will give us what we need to do the will of God, but only if we submit ourselves to him.

Revelation 3:20

20 "Look! Here I stand at the door and knock. If you hear me calling and open the door, I will come in, and we will share a meal as friends. 54

He will not break in; he will only come in if he's invited. If we resist him, he will leave. Here are the words that Stephen, the first martyr for Christ, spoke concerning resisting the Holy Spirit.

Acts 7:51

51 "You stubborn people! You are heathen at heart and deaf to the truth. Must you forever resist the Holy Spirit? But your ancestors did, and so do you! 55

53*The Contemporary English [computer file], electronic ed., Logos Library System*, (Nashville: Thomas Nelson) 1997, c1995 by the American Bible Society.
54*Holy Bible, New Living Translation*, (Wheaton, IL: Tyndale House Publishers, Inc.) 1996.
55*Holy Bible, New Living Translation*, (Wheaton, IL: Tyndale House Publishers, Inc.) 1996.

So how do we resist the Holy Spirit? By ignoring the evidence of God, by rejecting the deity of Jesus, and by rejecting the call of the Holy Spirit. God revealed himself to man through the creation of the world, through the Word of God, and through the Holy Spirit. When we ignore the clear evidence of God we are resisting the Holy Spirit.

Psalm 19:1-3

1 The heavens tell of the glory of God. The skies display his marvelous craftsmanship. 2 Day after day they continue to speak; night after night they make him known. 3 They speak without a sound or a word; their voice is silent in the skies; 56

Romans 1:20-21

20 From the time the world was created, people have seen the earth and sky and all that God made. They can clearly see his invisible qualities—his eternal power and divine nature. So they have no excuse whatsoever for not knowing God. 21 Yes, they knew God, but they wouldn't worship him as God or even give him thanks. And they began to think up foolish ideas of what God was like. The result was that their minds became dark and confused. 57

The triune nature of God does not allow for us to accept one person of the Godhead without accepting the others. You can't accept God the Father (Jehovah), without accepting his Son Jesus. Neither can you truly embrace who Jesus is without walking in the power of the Holy Spirit.

56*Holy Bible, New Living Translation*, (Wheaton, IL: Tyndale House Publishers, Inc.) 1996.

57*Holy Bible, New Living Translation*, (Wheaton, IL: Tyndale House Publishers, Inc.) 1996.

John 14:6

6 Jesus told him, "I am the way, the truth, and the life. No one can come to the Father except through me. 58

1 John 5:7

7 For there are three that bear record in heaven, the Father, the Word, and the Holy Ghost: and these three are one. 59

In the book of Matthew, verses 13-18 of the 16th chapter, Jesus asked his disciples who they thought he was. Peter spoke and said he was the Christ, son of the living God. Jesus then said no man revealed that to you, but my father, which is in heaven. Jesus then declared that this would be the method in which his church would be built. The method is the revelation of who Jesus is from the Spirit of God. Revelations 3:20 indicate to us that the Spirit of God stands at the door of our heart and knocks. He waits for us to accept him. If we reject the calling of Holy Spirit, then we cannot know God.

Hebrews 3:15

15 But never forget the warning: "Today you must listen to his voice. Don't harden your hearts against him as Israel did when they rebelled." 60

58*Holy Bible, New Living Translation*, (Wheaton, IL: Tyndale House Publishers, Inc.) 1996.

59*The King James Version*, (Cambridge: Cambridge) 1769.

60*Holy Bible, New Living Translation*, (Wheaton, IL: Tyndale House Publishers, Inc.) 1996.

Everyday Questions & Answers

As a pastor, I've been asked many questions concerning the Holy Spirit. It has let me know that there are a lot of people with a lot of unanswered questions on this subject. In my quest to learn more about the Holy Spirit and gain the answers to these questions, I realized that the answers could not be based on what I've heard, or even what I thought; but they had to be based on what the Holy Bible actually said. And if the Holy Bible was quiet on a particular subject, I could not insert my own opinion. All the answers that are given to the questions that follow are biblically based with scripture references.

When do you receive the Holy Spirit?

This question assumes that there are two separate events that happen in the life of a Christian. One is that he or she gets saved, and the other is that he or she receives the Holy Spirit. But are these two separate events really supported by the Word of God?

Ephesians 1:13

13 In whom ye also trusted, after that ye heard the word of truth, the gospel of your salvation: in whom also after that ye believed, ye were sealed with that Holy Spirit of promise, 61

This passage would indicate that at the moment one believes in Christ (becomes saved), he becomes sealed with the Holy Spirit. If you look at this same passage in the New Living Translation, it makes this point even clearer:

---

61 *The King James Version*, (Cambridge: Cambridge) 1769.

Ephesians 1:13

13 And now you also have heard the truth, the Good News that God saves you. And when you believed in Christ, he identified you as his own by giving you the Holy Spirit, whom he promised long ago. 62

At the very moment of accepting Christ, he accepts us as his own, and identifies or seals us as his through the Holy Spirit. As a matter of fact, there are several scriptures that indicated that we must have the Holy Spirit in order to be saved.

Romans 8:9

9 But ye are not in the flesh, but in the Spirit, if so be that the Spirit of God dwell in you. Now if any man have not the Spirit of Christ, he is none of his. 63

Now look at this same verse in the contemporary version:

Romans 8:9

9 But you are not controlled by your sinful nature. You are controlled by the Spirit if you have the Spirit of God living in you. (And remember that those who do not have the Spirit of Christ living in them are not Christians at all.) 64

This is not my opinion; this is a passage in the Holy Bible that clearly states that if we do not have the Holy Spirit,

62*Holy Bible, New Living Translation*, (Wheaton, IL: Tyndale House Publishers, Inc.) 1996.
63*The King James Version*, (Cambridge: Cambridge) 1769.
64*Holy Bible, New Living Translation*, (Wheaton, IL: Tyndale House Publishers, Inc.) 1996.

we do not belong to Christ. An individual may still be a babe in Christ, not demonstrating the life of a mature Christian, but in order to accept Christ, they have to have the Holy Spirit.

Revelation 3:20

20 Behold, I stand at the door, and knock: if any man hear my voice, and open the door, I will come in to him, and will sup with him, and he with me. 65

The picture painted here by Christ himself is that the Holy Spirit comes to live in us when we open up the doors of our heart. The moment we accept Christ, the Holy Spirit comes to live in us. There is no waiting period, no begging period, no tarrying period. A person receives the Holy Spirit the very moment they accept Christ and believe in him according to Romans 10:9.

Romans 10:9

9 For if you confess with your mouth that Jesus is Lord and believe in your heart that God raised him from the dead, you will be saved. 66

Have you received the Holy Ghost since you believed?

This question is one that comes from the Holy Bible directly. On the surface of things, it would indicate that a person could believe and not have the Holy Spirit.

Acts 19:2

65*The King James Version*, (Cambridge: Cambridge) 1769.
66*Holy Bible, New Living Translation*, (Wheaton, IL: Tyndale House Publishers, Inc.) 1996.

2 He said unto them, Have ye received the Holy Ghost since ye believed? And they said unto him, We have not so much as heard whether there be any Holy Ghost. 67

Thus many have taken this passage to mean that we could be saved and not have the Holy Spirit. However, the reality is that the people referred to in this passage were not truly saved:

Acts 19:3

3 And he said unto them, Unto what then were ye baptized? And they said, Unto John's baptism. 68

These men were "John the Baptist" disciples who had not come into the knowledge of Christ. They couldn't have been saved because Christ is the only way to God. Jesus is the only name whereby men may be saved. The moment you accept Christ, the Holy Spirit comes to live in you, seal you, and baptize you into the body of believers. Paul recognized that this had not happened to these people, and thus explained to them what it meant to be saved in the next verses.

Acts 19:4-5

4 Then said Paul, John verily baptized with the baptism of repentance, saying unto the people, that they should believe on him which should come after him, that is, on Christ Jesus. 5 When they heard this, they were baptized in the name of the Lord Jesus. 69

Once they accepted the message of Jesus Christ, they became saved and received the Holy Spirit.

67*The King James Version*, (Cambridge: Cambridge) 1769.
68*The King James Version*, (Cambridge: Cambridge) 1769.
69*The King James Version*, (Cambridge: Cambridge) 1769.

Acts 19:6-7

6 And when Paul had laid his hands upon them, the Holy Ghost came on them; and they spake with tongues, and prophesied. 7 And all the men were about twelve. 70

Now please note that once they accepted Jesus Christ, they received the Holy Spirit. The reason these men did not have the Holy Spirit before was not because they needed to tarry or wait for him, it was because they had not accepted Jesus Christ as their Savior.

Do you lose the Holy Spirit when you sin?

This is a very powerful question. It boils down to "What happens when we sin?" The incorrect answer to this question is responsible for a lot of people not being saved or in the church today! The way I answer this question is to first look at how we received the Holy Spirit.

If you recall, we receive the Holy Spirit at the moment we accept Christ according to Ephesians 1:13 and Revelations 3:20. Let's look at both of these scriptures again:

Ephesians 1:13

13 In whom ye also trusted, after that ye heard the word of truth, the gospel of your salvation: in whom also after that ye believed, ye were sealed with that Holy Spirit of promise, 71

Revelation 3:20

---

70 *The King James Version*, (Cambridge: Cambridge) 1769.
71 *The King James Version*, (Cambridge: Cambridge) 1769.

20 Behold, I stand at the door, and knock: if any man hear my voice, and open the door, I will come in to him, and will sup with him, and he with me. 72

What I want you to notice in looking at these scriptures is that there is no mention of sin. In other words, the Holy Bible never says for us to give up sin in order to receive the Holy Spirit. Don't misunderstand my position concerning sin. I'm not an advocate of the "once saved always saved" doctrine! As a matter of fact, God clearly does not want us to sin. He hates all sin.

Romans 6:1-2

What shall we say then? Shall we continue in sin, that grace may abound? 2 God forbid. How shall we, that are dead to sin, live any longer therein? 73

We were saved not because we stopped sinning, but because of God's grace. We were justified in the sight of God through the death of Jesus on the cross, and thus receive the gift of Salvation and the gift of the Holy Spirit. Our lack of sinning did not save us and cannot save us. As a matter of fact, God says that any righteousness that we could muster up would be as filthy rags to him anyway.

Isaiah 64:6

6 All of us have become like one who is unclean, and all our righteous acts are like filthy rags;
we all shrivel up like a leaf, and like the wind our sins sweep us away. 74

72*The King James Version*, (Cambridge: Cambridge) 1769.
73*The King James Version*, (Cambridge: Cambridge) 1769.
74*The New International Version*, (Grand Rapids, MI: Zondervan Publishing House) 1984.

A gift is something that one receives free of charge. If we had to work for the Holy Spirit, then it would no longer be a gift. If I tell you I'm going to give you a gift of one hundred dollars, but then ask you first to clean my house before I give it you; then the hundred dollars is no longer a gift, but a wage for services rendered. We do not earn the Holy Spirit because he is not a wage; he's a gift. As a matter of fact, there is not enough we could ever do to earn the Holy Spirit. So God gave us the Holy Spirit as a gift. The Holy Spirit did not come to us because we stopped sinning, he came to us because we accepted God's gift of salvation.

Jeremiah 3:14

14 Turn, O backsliding children, saith the LORD; for I am married unto you: and I will take you one of a city, and two of a family, and I will bring you to Zion: 75

The Holy Spirit lives in us so that he can lead us, guide us, and teach us all things. A teacher is there to teach you not just when you do things right, but also when you make mistakes. If the Holy Spirit left us every time we sinned, how could he ever teach us? Now here is what is suppose to happen when we sin:

1 John 2:1-2

1 My dear children, I am writing this to you so that you will not sin. But if you do sin, there is someone to plead for you before the Father. He is Jesus Christ, the one who pleases God completely. 2 He is the sacrifice for our sins. He takes away not only our sins but the sins of all the world. 76

75*The King James Version*, (Cambridge: Cambridge) 1769.
76*Holy Bible, New Living Translation*, (Wheaton, IL: Tyndale House Publishers, Inc.) 1996.

Sin does not forfeit us from the Holy Spirit no more than a child is forfeited from his family when he misbehaves. But when that child is bad, he simply says to his parents "I'm sorry"! And so it is with us as Christians. If we sin, we simply say to the father "I'm sorry"!

What does it mean to be filled with the Holy Spirit?

In the section titled "When does a person receive the Holy Spirit", we learned that the Holy Spirit enters our heart when we accept Christ. As a matter of fact, according to Romans 8:9, we do not belong to Christ unless we have the Holy Spirit. But this question deals with the filling of the Holy Spirit. I believe that a person can have the Holy Spirit and yet not be filled with the Holy Spirit. To be filled with the Holy Spirit simply means to be totally controlled by the Holy Spirit.

Ephesians 5:18

18 And be not drunk with wine, wherein is excess; but be filled with the Spirit; 77

The New Living Translation actually uses the word "control" when referring to being filled with the Holy Spirit.

Ephesians 5:18

18 Don't be drunk with wine, because that will ruin your life. Instead, let the Holy Spirit fill and control you. 78

77*The King James Version*, (Cambridge: Cambridge) 1769.
78*Holy Bible, New Living Translation*, (Wheaton, IL: Tyndale House Publishers, Inc.) 1996.

This passage in the Holy Bible uses a metaphor to describe what it means to be filled with the Holy Spirit. It first says be not drunk with wine! When a person is drunk with wine, the wine controls them. They begin to do things that they would not ordinarily do. A quiet and reserved person all of a sudden becomes the life of the party or very rowdy. The wine is now controlling their behavior. So what this scripture is saying is that when you are filled with the Holy Spirit, he will control your behavior. You will begin to do things that you would not have ordinarily done. For example, Jesus says that we should love our enemies. Well most people, saved or unsaved, are incapable of doing this. But when you are filled with the Holy Spirit, you can!

Now if you recognize being filled with the Holy Spirit as being controlled by the Holy Spirit, it would explain why the behavior of some Christians differs from that of others. The Holy Bible supports this concept and calls it being a babe in Christ.

1 Corinthians 3:1-3

And I, brethren, could not speak unto you as unto spiritual, but as unto carnal, even as unto babes in Christ. 2 I have fed you with milk, and not with meat: for hitherto ye were not able to bear it, neither yet now are ye able. 3 For ye are yet carnal: for whereas there is among you envying, and strife, and divisions, are ye not carnal, and walk as men? 79

Now look at the third verse in the New Living Translation:

1 Corinthians 3:3

79*The King James Version*, (Cambridge: Cambridge) 1769.

3 for you are still controlled by your own sinful desires. You are jealous of one another and quarrel with each other. Doesn't that prove you are controlled by your own desires? You are acting like people who don't belong to the Lord. 80

Please note that a babe in Christ is not necessarily a person that just got saved. It is a person who is not being controlled by the Spirit, but by their sinful, fleshly desires. We move from being a babe in Christ to being a mature Christian when the Holy Spirit is controlling us. But also please note that a Christian filled with the Holy Spirit can move back into being a babe in Christ if they allow their sinful nature to move back into control of their lives. This is why I say that being filled with the Holy Spirit is not a one-time event signified by speaking in tongues or some other outward event, but by the ongoing demonstration of a lifestyle controlled by the Spirit. And just as a car must constantly go and get filled with gas, we must do the things necessary to constantly get filled with the Holy Spirit.

How do you become filled with the Holy Spirit?

From the previous section, we learned that to be filled with the Holy Spirit means to be controlled by the Holy Spirit. So what does a person do to become filled or controlled by the Holy Spirit?

I have heard some well-meaning Christians say that you simply seek God for the filling of the Holy Spirit, and that at some timeframe, only known by God himself, he will fill you and you will begin speaking in tongues. But this is not

---

80*Holy Bible, New Living Translation*, (Wheaton, IL: Tyndale House Publishers, Inc.) 1996.

biblically supported, and it does not follow the definition of what it means to be filled. As a matter of fact, I've seen people speak in tongues the very first time they accept Christ, and then never come back to Church. Were they filled? I've also seen other people speak in tongues on Sunday morning, and then curse you out Sunday night! Were they filled? I've also seen others speak in tongues during a Spirit filled service, having just committed fornication earlier that day. Were they filled? Of course not! The Holy Spirit was clearly not controlling their lives.

There are a series of steps we must follow to become filled with the Holy Spirit. But again, please recognize that being filled is not a one-time event that one accomplishes after a certain amount of time or after doing a certain series of things. Being filled is an everyday ongoing process! The more we do the process, the more we are filled with the Holy Spirit, and thus the more we become like Christ. However, if we stop the process, we will become less like Christ, losing the infilling of the Holy Spirit.

Eight steps to becoming filled with the Holy Spirit

I've identified eight steps necessary for every Christian to become filled with the Holy Spirit. By no means are these steps conclusive, but if we do them, they will help us to allow the Holy Spirit to control our lives.

The first step is to submit to the Holy Spirit:

Matthew 16:24

24 Then said Jesus unto his disciples, If any man will come after me, let him deny himself, and take up his cross, and follow me. 81

Simply put, let the ways of the Lord become first in your life. Deny your desires and submit yourself to the ways of the Lord.

The second step is to pray for conviction:

Psalm 139:23-24

23 Search me, O God, and know my heart: try me, and know my thoughts: 24 And see if there be any wicked way in me, and lead me in the way everlasting. 82

The Holy Bible lets us know that our hearts are deceitful and wicked. We can't even trust our own heart (how we feel or what we think). So in order for us to learn the right things to do in our hearts, we must pray to God for conviction. I may feel that a certain behavior is perfectly acceptable, but if I pray to God, the Holy Spirit will convict me if the behavior is not acceptable to him.

The third step is to allow the Holy Spirit to guide you:

John 16:13

13 Howbeit when he, the Spirit of truth, is come, he will guide you into all truth: for he shall not speak of himself; but whatsoever he shall hear, that shall he speak: and he will shew you things to come. 83

Matthew 6:13

---

81 *The King James Version*, (Cambridge: Cambridge) 1769.
82 *The King James Version*, (Cambridge: Cambridge) 1769.
83 *The King James Version*, (Cambridge: Cambridge) 1769.

13 And lead us not into temptation, but deliver us from evil: For thine is the kingdom, and the power, and the glory, for ever. Amen. 84

Many times people fall into temptations or miss out on the blessings of the Lord because they are in the wrong place at the wrong time. The Holy Spirit is here to lead us away from temptations and lead us into God's purpose for our lives.

The fourth step is to become obedient to the Holy Spirit:

Galatians 5:16

16 This I say then, Walk in the Spirit, and ye shall not fulfil the lust of the flesh. 85

The Holy Bible indicates that we can grieve and quench the Holy Spirit. We grieve him when we engage in sinful behavior, and we quench him when we do not do the things he wants us to do. This is being disobedient. We must become obedient to the Holy Spirit in our behavior.

The fifth step is to study God's Word:

Psalm 119:11

11 Thy word have I hid in mine heart, that I might not sin against thee. 86

Psalm 1:1-2

Blessed is the man that walketh not in the counsel of the ungodly, nor standeth in the way of sinners, nor sitteth in

---

84*The King James Version*, (Cambridge: Cambridge) 1769.
85*The King James Version*, (Cambridge: Cambridge) 1769.
86*The King James Version*, (Cambridge: Cambridge) 1769.

the seat of the scornful. 2 But his delight is in the law of the LORD; and in his law doth he meditate day and night. 87

Because we are incapable of knowing the ways of the Lord, we must study his Word in order to learn his ways.

The sixth step is to develop a new lifestyle:

1 Thessalonians 5:16-22

16 Rejoice evermore. 17 Pray without ceasing. 18 In every thing give thanks: for this is the will of God in Christ Jesus concerning you. 19 Quench not the Spirit. 20 Despise not prophesyings. 21 Prove all things; hold fast that which is good. 22 Abstain from all appearance of evil. 88

I pray everyday at 6:00am. I didn't always do this, but now I do. I have found that it has revolutionized my walk with Christ. Although I didn't always pray like this, it became a lifestyle that I learned and adopted. Some people may think that praying like this is too much, but I say it is simply a lifestyle change. Most people get up everyday to go to work. They didn't do this all their life, but they adopted that lifestyle so that they could pay their bills. If we can learn and adopt a lifestyle of working everyday to pay bills, then we can learn and adopt a lifestyle that is necessary for us to become filled with the Holy Spirit.

The seventh step is to transform your mind:

Romans 12:1-2

I beseech you therefore, brethren, by the mercies of God, that ye present your bodies a living sacrifice, holy,

---

87*The King James Version,* (Cambridge: Cambridge) 1769.
88*The King James Version,* (Cambridge: Cambridge) 1769.

acceptable unto God, which is your reasonable service. 2 And be not conformed to this world: but be ye transformed by the renewing of your mind, that ye may prove what is that good, and acceptable, and perfect, will of God. 89

In order to be filled by the Holy Spirit (controlled by the Holy Spirit) we have to transform our old minds to new ones. Our mind represents what we think, what we do, and how we feel. It has to be transformed into thinking what God wants us to think, what God wants us to do, and how God wants us to feel. This happens when we follow the instructions of verses 9-20 of the 12th chapter of Romans.

Romans 12:9-20

9 Don't just pretend that you love others. Really love them. Hate what is wrong. Stand on the side of the good. 10 Love each other with genuine affection, and take delight in honoring each other. 11 Never be lazy in your work, but serve the Lord enthusiastically. 12 Be glad for all God is planning for you. Be patient in trouble, and always be prayerful. 13 When God's children are in need, be the one to help them out. And get into the habit of inviting guests home for dinner or, if they need lodging, for the night. 14 If people persecute you because you are a Christian, don't curse them; pray that God will bless them. 15 When others are happy, be happy with them. If they are sad, share their sorrow. 16 Live in harmony with each other. Don't try to act important, but enjoy the company of ordinary people. And don't think you know it all! 17 Never pay back evil for evil to anyone. Do things in such a way that everyone can see you are honorable. 18 Do your part to live in peace with everyone, as much as possible. 19 Dear friends, never avenge yourselves. Leave that to God. For it is written,

---

89*The King James Version*, (Cambridge: Cambridge) 1769.

*"I will take vengeance; I will repay those who deserve it,"
says the Lord. 20 Instead, do what the Scriptures say: "If your
enemies are hungry, feed them. If they are thirsty, give them
something to drink, and they will be ashamed of what they
have done to you." 90*

The eighth step is to fast:

Mark 9:29

*29 And he said unto them, This kind can come forth by
nothing, but by prayer and fasting. 91*

To fast is to deny the natural, fleshly, sinful body, and
develop a disciplined mind that is obedient to the Holy Spirit.
There are some things that will only be achieved by us when
we develop a lifestyle of prayer and fasting.

Again, these eight steps are not the only things we
must do as Christians to become filled with the Holy Spirit,
but they are a good start!

What's evidence of being filled with the Holy Spirit?

Evidence means to provide proof, to exhibit, or to
illustrate. I have always said that the evidence of an apple tree
is not in how gifted it is (how big, how beautiful, or how many
branches it has), but in the fruit it produces. The tree can be
the smallest, scrawniest tree in the orchard, but if it produces
just one apple, then it is an apple tree.

90*Holy Bible, New Living Translation*, (Wheaton, IL: Tyndale House
Publishers, Inc.) 1996.
91*The King James Version*, (Cambridge: Cambridge) 1769.

So then the evidence that a person is filled with (being controlled by) the Holy Spirit should be the fruit of the Spirit that is being produced in his or her life, as opposed to the gifts of the Spirit that may be in operation. I will deal more with fruit and gifts of the Holy Spirit in later chapters, but there must be some discussion here so that we can truly understand evidence. Let's look at two passages concerning gifts and fruit of the Spirit.

1 Corinthians 12:7-10

7 But the manifestation of the Spirit is given to every man to profit withal. 8 For to one is given by the Spirit the word of wisdom; to another the word of knowledge by the same Spirit; 9 To another faith by the same Spirit; to another the gifts of healing by the same Spirit; 10 To another the working of miracles; to another prophecy; to another discerning of spirits; to another divers kinds of tongues; to another the interpretation of tongues: 92

Galatians 5:22-23

22 But the fruit of the Spirit is love, joy, peace, longsuffering, gentleness, goodness, faith, 23 Meekness, temperance: against such there is no law. 93

Going back to our apple tree analogy, the purpose of an apple tree is not to be a gifted tree, but to produce apples. Who cares how beautiful and tall (i.e. gifted) an apple tree is if it does not produce apples. Then the purpose of the Holy Spirit in the life of a Christian is not to demonstrate gifts, but to produce fruit. Look at what Jesus said concerning fruit:

John 15:1-2

92*The King James Version*, (Cambridge: Cambridge) 1769.
93*The King James Version*, (Cambridge: Cambridge) 1769.

67

*I am the true vine, and my Father is the husbandman. 2
Every branch in me that beareth not fruit he taketh away: and
every branch that beareth fruit, he purgeth it, that it may bring
forth more fruit. 94*

Notice here that the focus is not put on gifts but on
fruit. Jesus did not say every branch that does not demonstrate
gifts (i.e. speaking in tongues) would be taken away; but every
branch that does not produce fruit.

The Holy Bible tells us that the fruit of the Spirit is
love, joy, peace, longsuffering, gentleness, goodness, faith,
meekness, and temperance. The evidence that a Christian is
filled with (controlled by) the Holy Spirit is when he or she is
demonstrating the fruit. I've often said that as a pastor I'd
rather have a church full of Christians demonstrating love, joy,
and peace who never speak in tongues, than to have a church
full of tongue speakers who are mean as the devil. And you
know what, I believe so would Christ. Our mission is to draw
sinners to Christ, and we cannot do that through speaking in
tongues, but we can do it through showing the love of God.

What's the purpose of the gifts of the Spirit?

Contrary to popular belief, the purpose of the gifts of
the Holy Spirit are not to demonstrate that we are filled with
the Holy Spirit. They are supernatural gifts given to
Christians to make the body of Christ stronger. This strength
would then enable the body of Christ to produce fruit. The
fruit would then attract sinners to Christ. We are going to
study Gifts of the Spirit in more detail in later chapters, but let
us look at a passage of scriptures that support the purpose of
these gifts.

94*The King James Version*, (Cambridge: Cambridge) 1769.

Ephesians 4:11-12

11 And he gave some, apostles; and some, prophets; and some, evangelists; and some, pastors and teachers; 12 For the perfecting of the saints, for the work of the ministry, for the edifying of the body of Christ: 95

The perfecting of the saints here means to learn how to serve or become servants for Christ. The edifying of the body of Christ means to make the body of Christ stronger. So then the purpose of the gifts are not to demonstrate to others that we have the Holy Spirit, but to make the body of Christ stronger.

Should every Christian speak in tongues?

I could very easily answer this question with a yes or no answer, but instead we will look and see exactly what the Holy Bible says about the subject. The answer will then not be based on my opinion, your opinion, or even the opinion of a particular church or denomination. The answer will be based solely on what God said in his Word.

The first point we must establish is that speaking in tongues is one of the many gifts that the Holy Spirit gives us when we accept Christ. Let us look again at the 12th chapter of 1 Corinthians; this time from the New Living Translation:

1 Corinthians 12:7-10

7 A spiritual gift is given to each of us as a means of helping the entire church. 8 To one person the Spirit gives the ability to give wise advice; to another he gives the gift of special knowledge. 9 The Spirit gives special faith to another,

---

95*The King James Version*, (Cambridge: Cambridge) 1769.

and to someone else he gives the power to heal the sick. 10 He gives one person the power to perform miracles, and to another the ability to prophesy. He gives someone else the ability to know whether it is really the Spirit of God or another spirit that is speaking. Still another person is given the ability to speak in unknown languages, and another is given the ability to interpret what is being said. 96

Notice here that this passage indicates that spiritual gifts are given to each of us to help the church. But also notice that everyone is not given the same gift. It is because we are a body, and each member of the body has a different purpose. The gifts are given to each of us so that we can accomplish our specified purpose to help the body become stronger. The 12th chapter of Romans also brings this point out!

Romans 12:3-6

3 For I say, through the grace given unto me, to every man that is among you, not to think of himself more highly than he ought to think; but to think soberly, according as God hath dealt to every man the measure of faith. 4 For as we have many members in one body, and all members have not the same office: 5 So we, being many, are one body in Christ, and every one members one of another. 6 Having then gifts differing according to the grace that is given to us, whether prophecy, let us prophesy according to the proportion of faith; 97

I think the New Living Translation of this passage of scriptures brings out this point even better:

96*Holy Bible, New Living Translation*, (Wheaton, IL: Tyndale House Publishers, Inc.) 1996.
97*The King James Version*, (Cambridge: Cambridge) 1769.

Romans 12:3-6

3 As God's messenger, I give each of you this warning: Be honest in your estimate of yourselves, measuring your value by how much faith God has given you. 4 Just as our bodies have many parts and each part has a special function, 5 so it is with Christ's body. We are all parts of his one body, and each of us has different work to do. And since we are all one body in Christ, we belong to each other, and each of us needs all the others. 6 God has given each of us the ability to do certain things well. So if God has given you the ability to prophesy, speak out when you have faith that God is speaking through you. 98

Now since both of these passages indicate that speaking in tongues is a gift from the Holy Spirit and that we are given different gifts, then we cannot be biblically correct if we say that every Christian has to have the gift of speaking in tongues. The Holy Bible even says that we all do not have the gift of speaking in tongues:

1 Corinthians 12:29-31

29 Is everyone an apostle? Of course not. Is everyone a prophet? No. Are all teachers? Does everyone have the power to do miracles? 30 Does everyone have the gift of healing? Of course not. Does God give all of us the ability to speak in unknown languages? Can everyone interpret unknown languages? No! 31 And in any event, you should desire the most helpful gifts. First, however, let me tell you about something else that is better than any of them! 99

98*Holy Bible, New Living Translation*, (Wheaton, IL: Tyndale House Publishers, Inc.) 1996.
99*Holy Bible, New Living Translation*, (Wheaton, IL: Tyndale House Publishers, Inc.) 1996.

The next point we must address is the passages in the Holy Bible that clearly indicate that people spoke in tongues when they were filled with the Holy Spirit. There are three of them: Acts 2:4, Acts 10:46, Acts 19:6. I will explain each of these passages and why these particular men spoke in tongues, but let us first answer another question. If God intended for everyone that was filled with the Holy Spirit to speak in tongues, then should not everyone in the Holy Bible that was filled, also speak in tongues? Well there were several people in the Holy Bible that were filled with the Holy Spirit with no record of them ever speaking in tongues.

Elisabeth, the mother of John the Baptist was filled with the Holy Spirit and we never see anywhere in the Holy Bible where she spoke in tongues.

Luke 1:41-42

41 And it came to pass, that, when Elisabeth heard the salutation of Mary, the babe leaped in her womb; and Elisabeth was filled with the Holy Ghost: 42 And she spake out with a loud voice, and said, Blessed art thou among women, and blessed is the fruit of thy womb. 100

John the Baptist himself was filled with the Holy Ghost, and there is also no record of him ever speaking in tongues.

Luke 1:15

15 For he shall be great in the sight of the Lord, and shall drink neither wine nor strong drink; and he shall be filled with the Holy Ghost, even from his mother's womb. 101

100*The King James Version*, (Cambridge: Cambridge) 1769.
101*The King James Version*, (Cambridge: Cambridge) 1769.

The apostle Paul received the Holy Ghost during his conversion. The Holy Bible tells us several things that happened during his conversion, but does not mention speaking in tongues as one of them. Although 1st Corinthians does indicate that Paul spoke in tongues, we see no evidence that he did it during his initial conversion when he was first filled.

Acts 9:17-18

17 So Ananias went and found Saul. He laid his hands on him and said, "Brother Saul, the Lord Jesus, who appeared to you on the road, has sent me so that you may get your sight back and be filled with the Holy Spirit." 18 Instantly something like scales fell from Saul's eyes, and he regained his sight. Then he got up and was baptized. 102

Jesus himself was filled with the Holy Spirit, and again we do not see him speaking in tongues:

Luke 4:1

And Jesus being full of the Holy Ghost returned from Jordan, and was led by the Spirit into the wilderness, 103

If the Holy Bible does not specifically say that everyone who is filled with the Holy Ghost must speak in tongues, then we should not make assumptions where the Holy Bible is silent.

Now let us address the three passages in the Holy Bible (there are only three) where the people spoke in tongues when they were filled with the Holy Spirit. It is not a

---

102*Holy Bible, New Living Translation*, (Wheaton, IL: Tyndale House Publishers, Inc.) 1996.
103*The King James Version*, (Cambridge: Cambridge) 1769.

coincidence that all three are in book of Acts during the formation of the first church of Christ. There was something special going on in each of these three passages of scripture, and the Holy Spirit chose to manifest himself in a special way. Let us take a look at each of them.

Acts 2:1-4

And when the day of Pentecost was fully come, they were all with one accord in one place. 2 And suddenly there came a sound from heaven as of a rushing mighty wind, and it filled all the house where they were sitting. 3 And there appeared unto them cloven tongues like as of fire, and it sat upon each of them. 4 And they were all filled with the Holy Ghost, and began to speak with other tongues, as the Spirit gave them utterance. 104

In an earlier chapter titled "The Introduction of the Holy Spirit", I explained this passage in great detail. The key point I brought out was that this passage was not instructional, but historical. The second chapter of Acts is not instructing us on what happens when we receive the Holy Spirit, it is giving us an historical account of what happened when these men received the Holy Spirit.

In Acts 2:1-4; these men received the supernatural gift of speaking in tongues to signify the introduction of the Holy Spirit dwelling in man. The Holy Spirit no longer needs to be introduced to man; he is already here. This explains the first passages, but what about the other two?

Acts 10:44-48

44 While Peter yet spake these words, the Holy Ghost fell on all them which heard the word. 45 And they of the

---

104*The King James Version,* (Cambridge: Cambridge) 1769.

circumcision which believed were astonished, as many as came with Peter, because that on the Gentiles also was poured out the gift of the Holy Ghost. 46 For they heard them speak with tongues, and magnify God. Then answered Peter, 47 Can any man forbid water, that these should not be baptized, which have received the Holy Ghost as well as we? 48 And he commanded them to be baptized in the name of the Lord. Then prayed they him to tarry certain days. 105

Jesus himself said he came for the lost sheep of the house of Israel. He was sent for the Jews (Matthew 15:24), but consequently adopted the Gentiles (Romans 8:15). Now when we study this second passage of Acts concerning speaking in tongues as a result of being filled with the Holy Spirit, we see that the individuals being referred to are Gentiles (Acts 10:45). When the Holy Spirit was first introduced to man in the 2nd chapter of Acts, those individuals were all Jews. In the 10th chapter of Acts, the Holy Spirit was introduced to the Gentiles in basically the same way he was introduced to the Jews. And Peter indicated this in the 47th verse when he stated, "Can anyone object to their being baptized, now that they have received the Holy Spirit just as we did?"

Now let us look at the third passage of scripture where we see the people speaking in tongues after receiving the Holy Spirit.

Acts 19:5-6

5 When they heard this, they were baptized in the name of the Lord Jesus. 6 And when Paul had laid his hands upon them, the Holy Ghost came on them; and they spake with tongues, and prophesied. 106

---

105 *The King James Version*, (Cambridge: Cambridge) 1769.
106 *The King James Version*, (Cambridge: Cambridge) 1769.

We also looked at this passage in an earlier chapter titled "Have you received the Holy Ghost since you believed". If you recall from this chapter, we learned that these individuals were "John the Baptist" disciples. They were in a sort of "limbo" state. They had left the Mosaic Law of the Jews, but had not accepted the new law of Christ. So here was a third group of individuals that had to be introduced to the Holy Spirit. And just as with the Jews and the Gentiles, these individuals were introduced to the Holy Spirit in a similar manner.

These three passages are the only passages in the Holy Bible where we see people speaking in tongues after receiving the Holy Spirit. By studying the context of each of them, we see that these passages are not instructions for the modern Christian, but the telling of historical events that occurred during the formation and establishment of the first church. And just as every Christian doesn't have the ability to part the red sea as Moses did, neither does every Christian have the ability to speak in tongues as these Christians did. As a matter of fact, not only does the Holy Bible never say that we all should speak in tongues, it actually tells us that we will have different gifts.

Romans 12:6

6 God has also given each of us different gifts to use. If we can prophesy, we should do it according to the amount of faith we have. 107

107*The Contemporary English [computer file], electronic ed., Logos Library System,* (Nashville: Thomas Nelson) 1997, c1995 by the American Bible Society.

1 Corinthians 12:11

11 But it is the Spirit who does all this and decides which gifts to give to each of us. 108

1 Corinthians 12:27-30

27 Now you are the body of Christ, and each one of you is a part of it. 28 And in the church God has appointed first of all apostles, second prophets, third teachers, then workers of miracles, also those having gifts of healing, those able to help others, those with gifts of administration, and those speaking in different kinds of tongues. 29 Are all apostles? Are all prophets? Are all teachers? Do all work miracles? 30 Do all have gifts of healing? Do all speak in tongues? Do all interpret? 109

The answer to the rhetorical question "Do all speak in tongues?" is obviously NO!

Do you have to speak in tongues to edify yourself?

This question comes about as a result of improper interpretation of the 14th chapter of 1st Corinthians.

1 Corinthians 14:4-5

4 He that speaketh in an unknown tongue edifieth himself; but he that prophesieth edifieth the church. 5 I would that ye all spake with tongues, but rather that ye prophesied:

108*The Contemporary English [computer file], electronic ed., Logos Library System,* (Nashville: Thomas Nelson) 1997, c1995 by the American Bible Society.
109*The New International Version,* (Grand Rapids, MI: Zondervan Publishing House) 1984.

for greater is he that prophesieth than he that speaketh with tongues, except he interpret, that the church may receive edifying.110

I've heard people use this passage to say that it is necessary for us to speak in tongues so that we can edify ourselves. Well that's not exactly what this passage really says. It says "he" that speaks in tongues edifies (strengthens) himself. Notice the exact wording of "he" and not "all of us". When we look at a modern interpretation of this passage, we see that it is referring only to those who have the gift of speaking in tongues.

1 Corinthians 14:4-5

4 A person who speaks in tongues is strengthened personally in the Lord, but one who speaks a word of prophecy strengthens the entire church. 5 I wish you all had the gift of speaking in tongues, but even more I wish you were all able to prophesy. For prophecy is a greater and more useful gift than speaking in tongues, unless someone interprets what you are saying so that the whole church can get some good out of it. 111

This passage also supports the fact that all of us do not have the gift of speaking in tongues. In the 5th verse, Paul says, I wish all of you had the gift of speaking in tongues. Now if we all had the ability to speak in tongues, why would Paul wish that we all had it? The point here is clearly we all do not have the gift of speaking in tongues or the gift of prophecy. Paul is saying that if we all were going to have the same gift, it would be better for us to have the gift of prophecy rather than the gift of speaking in tongues.

110*The King James Version*, (Cambridge: Cambridge) 1769.
111*Holy Bible, New Living Translation*, (Wheaton, IL: Tyndale House Publishers, Inc.) 1996.

Does praying in the Spirit mean praying in tongues?

The Holy Bible speaks of praying in the Spirit in several passages.

Ephesians 6:18

18 Praying always with all prayer and supplication in the Spirit, and watching thereunto with all perseverance and supplication for all saints; 112

Ephesians 6:18

18 Pray at all times and on every occasion in the power of the Holy Spirit. Stay alert and be persistent in your prayers for all Christians everywhere. 113

"In the Spirit" means in the power of the Holy Spirit, or under the direction of the Holy Spirit. Although some people may speak in tongues while they are praying, praying in the Spirit does not mean praying in tongues. The Holy Bible never said that, and so we shouldn't. If the spirit of God is leading me to pray, then I'm praying in the Spirit regardless of tongues!

Another passage I've heard people use concerning praying in the Spirit is Romans 8:26:

Romans 8:26

112*The King James Version*, (Cambridge: Cambridge) 1769.
113*Holy Bible, New Living Translation*, (Wheaton, IL: Tyndale House Publishers, Inc.) 1996.

79

Likewise the Spirit also helpeth our infirmities: for we know not what we should pray for as we ought: but the Spirit itself maketh intercession for us with groanings which cannot be uttered. 114

Here the Holy Bible says that the Spirit prays for us through groanings. Now groanings mean to sigh without putting into words. Look at this same passage from the contemporary version:

Romans 8:26

26 In certain ways we are weak, but the Spirit is here to help us. For example, when we don't know what to pray for, the Spirit prays for us in ways that cannot be put into words. 115

This cannot be speaking in tongues, because speaking in tongues is uttering words. So again this passage is not referring to every Christian speaking in tongues.

114*The King James Version*, (Cambridge: Cambridge) 1769.
115*The Contemporary English [computer file], electronic ed., Logos Library System*, (Nashville: Thomas Nelson) 1997, c1995 by the American Bible Society.

Part 2 • Fruit of the Spirit

Where's the Fruit?

In man's quest to understand the Holy Spirit, a lot of attention has been placed on the gifts of the Holy Spirit. A lot of emphasis and attention has been given to things like prophesy, healing, miracles, speaking in tongues, and other gifts. These things are important, but certainly no more important than the fruit of the Holy Spirit.

Galatians 5:22-23

22 But the fruit of the Spirit is love, joy, peace, longsuffering, gentleness, goodness, faith, 23 Meekness, temperance: against such there is no law. 116

This chapter is dedicated to describing both the purpose and the importance of the fruit of the Holy Spirit. If a Christian is not producing and demonstrating the fruit of the Spirit, then when it comes to the purpose of God, they are ineffective.

To describe the importance of the fruit of the Spirit, we must also look at the gifts of the Spirit to use as a comparison. The gifts and fruit of the Spirit are two different things, and they are obtained in two different ways. Noting the distinction between the two is important because we must understand that we can have one without the other.

Fruit of the Spirit vs. Gifts of the Spirit

Romans 12:4-6

116*The King James Version*, (Cambridge: Cambridge) 1769.

4 For as we have many members in one body, and all members have not the same office: 5 So we, being many, are one body in Christ, and every one members one of another. 6 Having then gifts differing according to the grace that is given to us, whether prophecy, let us prophesy according to the proportion of faith; 117

The word "gifts" used in the 6th verse here has a Hebrew translation of "charisma". It means free gift; favor with which one receives without any merit of his own. The key word in this definition is "free"! You cannot work to receive a gift, because if you do, then it's no longer a gift, but becomes wages for work performed.

On the other hand, the word "fruit", as used in Galatians 5:22 concerning the fruit of the Spirit, has a Hebrew translation of "karpos". It means the fruit of trees, vines, or fields. Unlike gifts, which are free, fruit is earned from the labor of one's efforts. To get fruit, one has to plow the earth, plant seeds, water the ground, pull up weeds, make sure the plants get enough sun, and then after enough effort, the seeds will eventually produce fruit.

Have you ever wondered how it is that a person can prophesy a word from the Lord in church, and then not even speak to you the next day at the mall? Or maybe you have wondered how a person can speak in tongues all day long on Sunday morning, and curse you out Sunday night? I've personally seen a person operating in a spirit of exhortation during a spirit filled church service, and later found out that the person was in an adulterous affair. Most people would simply say these people are hypocrites. But I have a better explanation! I call it "Where's the Fruit?"

117*The King James Version*, (Cambridge: Cambridge) 1769.

A number of years ago, there was a commercial on television for a famous fast food restaurant that had a punch line of "Where's the Beef?". The premise of the commercial was that other fast food restaurants had huge hamburger buns that made it appear you were getting a large hamburger. But when you opened the bun, there would be a little small piece of meat. The little old lady in the commercial would then say, "Where's the beef?".

My explanation for the behavior described earlier is that we have Christians who have big buns but no meat. In other words, they got saved, received their spiritual gifts, but then did nothing to produce the spiritual fruit. The gifts of the Holy Spirit are given to us from the Holy Spirit when we accept Christ. The fruit of the Holy Spirit are produced when we go through the sanctification process described in the Holy Bible.

Paul used the first five chapters of the book of Romans to teach us that salvation was not a result of our efforts, but a result of God's grace. Our salvation came through the efforts of Jesus Christ.

Romans 3:24

24 Being justified freely by his grace through the redemption that is in Christ Jesus: 118

Romans 5:21

21 That as sin hath reigned unto death, even so might grace reign through righteousness unto eternal life by Jesus Christ our Lord. 119

118*The King James Version*, (Cambridge: Cambridge) 1769.
119*The King James Version*, (Cambridge: Cambridge) 1769.

The key words in these verses are "justified", "freely", and "grace". We are justified by the redemptive work of Jesus Christ, which he gives to us as a free gift. All we have to do is accept it.

But in the 6th chapter of the book of Romans, Paul begins to talk about the importance of living a life that moves beyond God's grace.

Romans 6:1-2

What shall we say then? Shall we continue in sin, that grace may abound? 2 God forbid. How shall we, that are dead to sin, live any longer therein? 120

Paul says here, just because we have been given God's gift of salvation, we still need to do every thing we can to walk in the fruit of his Spirit, which is freeing ourselves from the chains of sin.

I have this little motto that I use when it comes to gifts vs. fruit: "Gifts are given, Fruit is earned!" People can prophesy, speak in tongues, heal bodies of illnesses, and perform miracles as a result of the gifts that were given to them by the Holy Spirit. However, people can only demonstrate supernatural love, joy, peace, and patience when they do the work necessary for the Holy Spirit to produce his fruit in their lives. Since getting the gifts of the Spirit is a different process than getting the fruit of the Spirit, then it's possible for Christians to have their free gifts and not have any fruit. This then is how a person can speak in tongues and still be one of the meanest persons in the church.

120*The King James Version*, (Cambridge: Cambridge) 1769.

"Perpetrating"

When we see a Christian involved in behavior inconsistent with being saved, we are quick to call them hypocrites. But if the behavior stems from a lack of fruit of the Spirit, I think a better word for them would be "Perpetrators". This may seem like I'm splitting hairs, but I believe the difference is significance. From a spiritual perspective, a hypocrite is a person in church pretending to be saved, and knows in their heart that they are not. A perpetrator on the other hand, really does believe that he or she is ok, but has a lifestyle that prevents them from winning others to Christ. They have no fruit!

If a woman is driving a new BMW and has an expensive Gucci bag on her arm, you would assume that she is prosperous. Now if you are in need, you may be tempted to follow her home and ask her for some help. You may pass up other opportunities for help because you feel that this woman can help you. But as you follow her home, you see that she lives in government project housing. I call this person a perpetrator. She was perpetrating to be a prosperous person, but she really was not. When we accept Christ and receive the gifts of the Holy Spirit, we are telling the world that we are Christians, and we have something that can help them. But if they follow us home and see no love, no joy, no peace, then we become perpetrators. And this may actually hurt the cause of Christ.

Matthew 21:18-19

18 Now in the morning as he returned into the city, he hungered. 19 And when he saw a fig tree in the way, he came to it, and found nothing thereon, but leaves only, and said unto it, Let no fruit grow on thee henceforward for ever. And presently the fig tree withered away. 121

Notice the symmetry in this passage of scriptures. We see Jesus hungry looking for something to eat. He sees a fig tree that from a distance appears to have fruit. But when he gets to it, he recognizes that there is no fruit. Well, the world is hungry and we are the light of the world (the ones with the fruit).

Matthew 5:14

14 Ye are the light of the world. A city that is set on an hill cannot be hid. 122

Matthew 11:28

28 Come unto me, all ye that labour and are heavy laden, and I will give you rest. 123

When you are hungry late a night, you look for the lights of a restaurant. If you find one, you will think that it's open and has food to satisfy your hunger. Now if after pulling into the restaurant, you find out that the restaurant has no food, you will be highly disappointed. This is what happens to the world when we as Christians indicate that we have what they need; however when they come to church, they find just as many problems in the church as out in the world. And this is what happened to Jesus in Matthew 21:19. He saw a fig tree from a distance with leaves on it. The leaves represented that it had fruit. But when he got to the tree, he found none. The world is looking for something to eat when they come to the church. They are looking for some fruit: love, joy, peace, longsuffering, gentleness, goodness, faith, meekness, and

---

121 *The King James Version*, (Cambridge: Cambridge) 1769.
122 *The King James Version*, (Cambridge: Cambridge) 1769.
123 *The King James Version*, (Cambridge: Cambridge) 1769.

temperance. We can have leaves (gifts of the Spirit), without having figs (fruit of the Spirit), but it will hurt the body of Christ. With the fig tree, Jesus cursed it because it could not satisfy his need. Now look at what Jesus said concerning the importance of us producing fruit:

John 15:1-2

I am the true vine, and my Father is the husbandman. 2 Every branch in me that beareth not fruit he taketh away: and every branch that beareth fruit, he purgeth it, that it may bring forth more fruit. 124

Your Relationship with God is based on your Fruit

In order for a flashlight to work, it must have a good battery. If it has a strong battery, it will produce a bright light. If it has a weak battery, it will produce a dim light. If it has a dead battery, it will produce no light. And so it is with us as Christians:

Matthew 5:16

16 Let your light so shine before men, that they may see your good works, and glorify your Father which is in heaven. 125

We are the flashlights to the world. But if our battery is not functioning properly, we will be ineffective. There are two reasons why a light will not shine bright from a flashlight: either the battery is weak, or the connectors to the battery are not working properly. Now our battery, the thing that makes

---

124*The King James Version*, (Cambridge: Cambridge) 1769.
125*The King James Version*, (Cambridge: Cambridge) 1769.

us shine bright to the world, is the Spirit of God. Since we know that the Spirit of God is everlasting, if we are not shining brightly, then the problem must be in us. And the way we determine if our connectors are good or bad is to determine what the Spirit is or is not producing in our lives; namely the fruit of the Spirit.

Galatians 5:22-23

22 But the fruit of the Spirit is love, joy, peace, longsuffering, gentleness, goodness, faith, 23 Meekness, temperance: against such there is no law. 126

Not only does the production of Spiritual Fruit affect our ability to be a light to the world, it also determines our relationship with God.

John 4:23-24

23 But the hour cometh, and now is, when the true worshippers shall worship the Father in spirit and in truth: for the Father seeketh such to worship him. 24 God is a Spirit: and they that worship him must worship him in spirit and in truth. 127

The only way we can have a true relationship with God is through the Spirit of God. Jesus says here in John 4:23 that this is what God is seeking. And the only way we can truly know that the Spirit is operating strongly in our lives is based on the fruit we are producing. When supernatural love, joy, peace, longsuffering, gentleness, goodness, faith, meekness, and temperance are being demonstrated in our lives, then we know that the Spirit is working very strongly. By

---

126*The King James Version*, (Cambridge: Cambridge) 1769.
127*The King James Version*, (Cambridge: Cambridge) 1769.

supernatural, I mean more or greater than what is humanly possible. Supernatural love is love that allows you to love your enemy. Supernatural joy is an inward joy that can be demonstrated outwardly even in the midst of great pain or sorrow. Supernatural peace is a peace of mind when all hell breaks loose and cannot be understood by the world. When we are producing fruit like this, we truly become the light to the world, and we in turn have a strong relationship with God through the Spirit.

Matthew 7:16-20

16 By their fruit you will recognize them. Do people pick grapes from thornbushes, or figs from thistles? 17 Likewise every good tree bears good fruit, but a bad tree bears bad fruit. 18 A good tree cannot bear bad fruit, and a bad tree cannot bear good fruit. 19 Every tree that does not bear good fruit is cut down and thrown into the fire. 20 Thus, by their fruit you will recognize them. 128

128*The New International Version*, (Grand Rapids, MI: Zondervan Publishing House) 1984.

Purpose and Expectations of Fruit

A preacher decided to go into the community to get to know the people. He began to play ball with a group at the park. They were unaware that he was a preacher because he did not wear a clergy's collar. One of the men intentionally bumped him, knocking him to the ground. Everyone began to laugh. Fighting to control his temper, the preacher got up and smiled dusting himself off. The one who had bumped him, noticed his good nature and began to help him up. His tormenter turned into his helper. As they talked, a connection was made, and they hung out after the game. He learned that the man, who looked down and out, had been a doctor, but because of alcohol, had lost both his practice and his family. The outcome of this story is that the preacher was able to lead him to Christ and eventually see him reunite with his family.[129]

Perhaps this is one of the purposes of the fruit of the Holy Spirit. If life was always kind, if people were always pleasant, if we never had headaches, if we never knew what it meant to be tired, if we were never under pressure, then the fruit of the Spirit might never get noticed.

It is during these difficulties and hardships that we especially need the fruit of the Spirit. And it is especially during such times as these that God works through us to touch other people for Christ. It's at those moments of truth, times of crisis, that the fruit of the Spirit kicks in as God intended, and accomplishes its purpose.

---

[129] Story from the book, Holy Spirit by Billy Graham

When people see the true fruit of the Spirit in us, they see Christ. And when they see him, they will be drawn to him!

John 12:32

32 And I, if I be lifted up from the earth, will draw all men unto me. 130

Jesus spent his life here on earth laying the foundation for the church. The church would be built upon Jesus himself. It would be built upon who he was. People would follow him because of what they saw in him. Jesus would spend three years training and teaching his disciples to be like him because he would soon leave.

John 14:25-27

25 These things have I spoken unto you, being yet present with you. 26 But the Comforter, which is the Holy Ghost, whom the Father will send in my name, he shall teach you all things, and bring all things to your remembrance, whatsoever I have said unto you. 27 Peace I leave with you, my peace I give unto you: not as the world giveth, give I unto you. Let not your heart be troubled, neither let it be afraid. 131

This passage of scripture explains how man would draw other men to Christ. First, Jesus would teach man while down on earth. Second, the Holy Spirit would teach man after Jesus ascended to heaven. Lastly he would give us peace, an element of the fruit of the Spirit. Armed with the Word of God and the fruit of the Spirit, man would be able to draw all men unto Christ.

130*The King James Version*, (Cambridge: Cambridge) 1769.
131*The King James Version*, (Cambridge: Cambridge) 1769.

So the purpose of the fruit of the Holy Spirit is to make man like Christ, enabling him to draw others. The expectation is then that man will learn God's Word and produce fruit, so that he can fulfill God's purpose. The purpose of a teacher is to teach the student. The expectation of the student is that he or she will learn. As Christians, we became students when we accepted Christ. God now expects us to learn his word and produce his fruit to draw others to him. If we are not doing this, then we are not meeting expectations.

James 1:22-24

22 But be ye doers of the word, and not hearers only, deceiving your own selves. 23 For if any be a hearer of the word, and not a doer, he is like unto a man beholding his natural face in a glass: 24 For he beholdeth himself, and goeth his way, and straightway forgetteth what manner of man he was. 132

It is God's expectation that we don't just hear about his word, but that we learn and do it. It is also his expectation that we also don't just hear about the fruit of the Spirit, but that we produce it.

Matthew 5:43-48

43 "You have heard that the law of Moses says, 'Love your neighbor' and hate your enemy. 44 But I say, love your enemies! Pray for those who persecute you! 45 In that way, you will be acting as true children of your Father in heaven. For he gives his sunlight to both the evil and the good, and he sends rain on the just and on the unjust, too. 46 If you love only those who love you, what good is that? Even corrupt tax collectors do that much. 47 If you are kind only to your

---

132*The King James Version*, (Cambridge: Cambridge) 1769.

friends, how are you different from anyone else? Even pagans do that. 48 But you are to be perfect, even as your Father in heaven is perfect. 133

It is when we produce fruit in unexpected situations that the world sees Christ in us. Anybody can produce love towards their friends, but the Holy Spirit can produce a love in us that will cause us to love our enemies.

Building a "Fenced" Garden

Now since we are expected to produce fruit of the Spirit in our lives, how are we to do it? Unlike gifts, which are given free of charge, fruit has to be earned and produced. When a person creates a garden, one of the things they will often do is build a fence around the garden to protect it. The fence has two purposes. It keeps the good things in and the bad things out.

Before we were saved, our lives were like an open field. Things came and went as they saw fit. It's very difficult to produce a garden in an open field. Animals will come trample on the seeds, preventing them from growing. Other animals will dig up the fruit that is trying to grow. To get a good garden, it is important that you build a fence around it for protection. When we accept Christ, we need to build a fence around us so that we can produce our fruit. The fence keeps out all the things that come to prevent our fruit from growing, or destroy our fruit while it is trying to grow. Once we get a good fenced garden, we are then able to produce much fruit.

133*Holy Bible, New Living Translation*, (Wheaton, IL: Tyndale House Publishers, Inc.) 1996.

John 15:8

8 Herein is my Father glorified, that ye bear much fruit; so shall ye be my disciples. 134

Spiritually speaking, our fence is our lifestyle. If we maintain the same lifestyle that we had before we were saved, then we will not have a fence that will allow us to produce fruit. So the Holy Bible teaches us to change our lifestyle, thereby removing the things that inhibit the production of Spiritual fruit.

Hebrews 12:1-2

1 Therefore, since we are surrounded by such a huge crowd of witnesses to the life of faith, let us strip off every weight that slows us down, especially the sin that so easily hinders our progress. And let us run with endurance the race that God has set before us. 2 We do this by keeping our eyes on Jesus, on whom our faith depends from start to finish. He was willing to die a shameful death on the cross because of the joy he knew would be his afterward. Now he is seated in the place of highest honor beside God's throne in heaven. 135

134*The King James Version*, (Cambridge: Cambridge) 1769.
135*Holy Bible, New Living Translation*, (Wheaton, IL: Tyndale House Publishers, Inc.) 1996.

Yielding! Faith and Works!

John 15:1-2

I am the true vine, and my Father is the husbandman. 2 Every branch in me that beareth not fruit he taketh away: and every branch that beareth fruit, he purgeth it, that it may bring forth more fruit. 136

When a branch is producing fruit, it is actually yielding fruit. So then one definition of yielding is to produce, earn, or bear. Another definition of yielding however is to relent, relinquish, or give up.

Both these definitions work hand in hand to give us the process necessary to produce the fruit of the Spirit. I call them "Yielding (producing) through Works" and "Yielding (giving up) through Faith".

As a little boy, I would go to apple orchards with my father to pick fruit every year. And every year these orchards would contain huge apple trees with lots of fruit on them. How did the farmer get these huge trees with lots of apples to grow on his farm year after year? Through the process of works and faith!

First the farmer "yielded through works" by planting seeds, applying fertilizer to the ground, pruning the branches, and pulling up weeds. However, none of this work actually made the trees grow, or the branches produce apples; it simply created the right environment for the trees to grow, and the fruit to be produced.

136*The King James Version*, (Cambridge: Cambridge) 1769.

We cannot make ourselves produce fruit of the Spirit through works, however we do have to create the right environment. Apple trees produced fruit because of something called the photosynthesis process of growth. The branches don't make themselves produce fruit; they yield themselves to this process. In other words, after the farmer has done his work to develop the proper environment for the fruit, he has to wait and have faith that the trees will grow and produce the apples. But if the farmer didn't do his work, there would be nothing for his faith to act upon!

Faith in God is yielding to God's will. But faith without works is dead. Expecting God to work without us first creating the proper environment is like the farmer expecting apples to be produced without him first working his orchard.

James 2:21-26

21 Was not Abraham our father justified by works, when he had offered Isaac his son upon the altar? 22 Seest thou how faith wrought with his works, and by works was faith made perfect? 23 And the scripture was fulfilled which saith, Abraham believed God, and it was imputed unto him for righteousness: and he was called the Friend of God. 24 Ye see then how that by works a man is justified, and not by faith only. 25 Likewise also was not Rahab the harlot justified by works, when she had received the messengers, and had sent them out another way? 26 For as the body without the spirit is dead, so faith without works is dead also. 137

So we produce fruit of the Spirit by yielding through works (doing our part), and then yielding through faith (allowing God to do his part).

137*The King James Version*, (Cambridge: Cambridge) 1769.

Mark 4:3-8

3 Hearken; Behold, there went out a sower to sow: 4 And it came to pass, as he sowed, some fell by the way side, and the fowls of the air came and devoured it up. 5 And some fell on stony ground, where it had not much earth; and immediately it sprang up, because it had no depth of earth: 6 But when the sun was up, it was scorched; and because it had no root, it withered away. 7 And some fell among thorns, and the thorns grew up, and choked it, and it yielded no fruit. 8 And other fell on good ground, and did yield fruit that sprang up and increased; and brought forth, some thirty, and some sixty, and some an hundred. 138

This good ground wasn't an accident; someone worked to produce it. The seeds had within them the ability to produce fruit, but couldn't until they were placed in good ground. And once they found good ground, they began to produce. The farmer produced the good ground and then yielded to faith.

Yielding through works (fasting, praying, studying God's Word, fellowshipping with other Christians) produces the good ground; yielding through faith (letting go of our will and trusting God's will) allows the Holy Spirit to then produce his fruit in us.

138*The King James Version*, (Cambridge: Cambridge) 1769.

Guarding Against Spiritual Anti-Fruit

One of the most important things we can do to help us in the production of the fruit of the Holy Spirit is to get rid of anything that inhibits its production.

Galatians 5:17

17 For the flesh lusteth against the Spirit, and the Spirit against the flesh: and these are contrary the one to the other: so that ye cannot do the things that ye would. 139

This passage says that our flesh works against the Spirit of God. Our flesh is contrary; it has an adversarial relationship to the Spirit of God. The Holy Spirit produces fruit of the Spirit; the flesh produces works of the flesh.

Galatians 5:19-21

19 Now the works of the flesh are manifest, which are these; Adultery, fornication, uncleanness, lasciviousness, 20 Idolatry, witchcraft, hatred, variance, emulations, wrath, strife, seditions, heresies, 21 Envyings, murders, drunkenness, revellings, and such like: of the which I tell you before, as I have also told you in time past, that they which do such things shall not inherit the kingdom of God. 140

"Anti" means anything that is against or contrary. "Anti-Christ" means anything or anyone that is against Christ. Therefore, "Anti-fruit" is anything that is against the production of the fruit of the Spirit. The Holy Bible calls

---

139*The King James Version*, (Cambridge: Cambridge) 1769.
140*The King James Version*, (Cambridge: Cambridge) 1769.

these things the "works of the flesh", and they are listed above in Galatians 5:19-21.

Ignorance is No Excuse of the Law

Have you ever seen someone try to plant a garden or have houseplants, but didn't know much about gardening? They may have had good intentions, but the end result is that the plants turned yellow and produced bad or no fruit. Thus regardless of the intentions, ignorance caused problems.

Hosea 4:6

6 My people are destroyed for lack of knowledge: because thou hast rejected knowledge, I will also reject thee, that thou shalt be no priest to me: seeing thou hast forgotten the law of thy God, I will also forget thy children. 141

Some of us are not producing good fruit because we are doing things out of ignorance that are contrary to producing good spiritual fruit. Perhaps you have heard the saying "What you don't know can't hurt you!" Well since it is our job to become like Christ and produce fruit, what we don't know can hurt us.

Vinegar is clear and looks just like water. Now if you are a gardener and use vinegar out of ignorance to water your plants, your seeds will die despite your good intentions. Because of your ignorance, no fruit will be produced in your garden. Likewise as Christians, we have an obligation to produce fruit in our spiritual garden. God has chosen us to produce fruit for the world, and we cannot afford to be ignorant in its production.

141*The King James Version*, (Cambridge: Cambridge) 1769.

2 Corinthians 2:11

11 Lest Satan should get an advantage of us: for we are not ignorant of his devices. 142

2 Timothy 2:15

15 Study to shew thyself approved unto God, a workman that needeth not to be ashamed, rightly dividing the word of truth. 143

Psalm 119:11

11 Thy word have I hid in mine heart, that I might not sin against thee. 144

Ignorance of the things that inhibit the production of spiritual fruit in our lives is no excuse. It's our job to study and learn God's Word so that we can rid ourselves of our anti-fruit.

There are three categories of anti-fruit that we must deal with if we want the Holy Spirit to produce fruit in our lives. These categories are called Sins Against the Body, Sins Against God, and Sins Against your Brother or Sister.

Anti-Fruit: Sins Against The Body

Galatians 5:19

142*The King James Version*, (Cambridge: Cambridge) 1769.
143*The King James Version*, (Cambridge: Cambridge) 1769.
144*The King James Version*, (Cambridge: Cambridge) 1769.

19 Now the works of the flesh are manifest, which are these; Adultery, fornication, uncleanness, lasciviousness, 145

Sins against the body are sins that deal with immorality, lust, and unbridled or unrestrained behavior (especially as it relates to sexual behavior). It's very easy to see how this anti-fruit can inhibit the Holy Spirit from producing spiritual fruit in our lives. Study the next passage of scripture.

1 Corinthians 6:15-20

15 Know ye not that your bodies are the members of Christ? shall I then take the members of Christ, and make them the members of an harlot? God forbid. 16 What? know ye not that he which is joined to an harlot is one body? for two, saith he, shall be one flesh. 17 But he that is joined unto the Lord is one spirit. 18 Flee fornication. Every sin that a man doeth is without the body; but he that committeth fornication sinneth against his own body. 19 What? know ye not that your body is the temple of the Holy Ghost which is in you, which ye have of God, and ye are not your own? 20 For ye are bought with a price: therefore glorify God in your body, and in your spirit, which are God's. 146

When we look at all the problems facing our society including racism, poverty, lack of education, crime, lack of opportunity, and more; the biggest detriment, however, is sexual immorality. This was also one of the biggest detriments to the children of Israel in the Holy Bible.

1 Corinthians 10:8

145*The King James Version*, (Cambridge: Cambridge) 1769.
146*The King James Version*, (Cambridge: Cambridge) 1769.

8 Neither let us commit fornication, as some of them committed, and fell in one day three and twenty thousand. 147

What is it that caused over 23,000 people to die in one day? Sexual immorality! But there is a related story to this passage that is even more interesting. You can find it in the Holy Bible if you study Numbers the 23rd, 24th, and 25th chapters. According to these chapters, a king by the name of Balak tried to pay a prophet by the name of Balaam to curse the children of Israel. But every time he tried to curse them, he ended up blessing them. The king became furious at Balaam because of this.

Numbers 24:10

10 King Balak flew into a rage against Balaam. He angrily clapped his hands and shouted, "I called you to curse my enemies! Instead, you have blessed them three times. 148

Balaam's response was "how can I curse something that God has blessed." He stated that he couldn't go against the will of God for any amount of money!

Numbers 24:13

13 'Even if Balak were to give me a palace filled with silver and gold, I am powerless to do anything against the will of the LORD.' I told you that I could say only what the LORD says! 149

147*The King James Version*, (Cambridge: Cambridge) 1769.
148*Holy Bible, New Living Translation*, (Wheaton, IL: Tyndale House Publishers, Inc.) 1996.
149*Holy Bible, New Living Translation*, (Wheaton, IL: Tyndale House Publishers, Inc.) 1996.

As Christians we must never lose sight of the fact that the Devil can't do anything to us that God doesn't allow. Balaam couldn't curse Israel because God wouldn't allow it. But by the time we get to the 25th chapter of Numbers, we see the children of Israel cursing themselves.

Numbers 25:1

While the Israelites were camped at Acacia, some of the men defiled themselves by sleeping with the local Moabite women. 150

This passage explains why over 23,000 children in Israel died in one day. It was because of sexual immorality.

Numbers 25:2-9

2 These women invited them to attend sacrifices to their gods, and soon the Israelites were feasting with them and worshiping the gods of Moab. 3 Before long Israel was joining in the worship of Baal of Peor, causing the LORD's anger to blaze against his people. 4 The LORD issued the following command to Moses: "Seize all the ringleaders and execute them before the LORD in broad daylight, so his fierce anger will turn away from the people of Israel." 5 So Moses ordered Israel's judges to execute everyone who had joined in worshiping Baal of Peor. 6 Just then one of the Israelite men brought a Midianite woman into the camp, right before the eyes of Moses and all the people, as they were weeping at the entrance of the Tabernacle. 7 When Phinehas son of Eleazar and grandson of Aaron the priest saw this, he jumped up and left the assembly. Then he took a spear 8 and rushed after the man into his tent. Phinehas thrust the spear all the way

---

150*Holy Bible, New Living Translation*, (Wheaton, IL: Tyndale House Publishers, Inc.) 1996.

through the man's body and into the woman's stomach. So the plague against the Israelites was stopped, 9 but not before 24,000 people had died. 151

All of this started from sexual immorality! Satan couldn't curse the children of Israel, but they could curse themselves because of Sins Against the Body.

Anti-Fruit: Sins Against God

Sins against God are the second set of anti-fruit that inhibits the Holy Spirit from producing his fruit in us. These sins are listed in the first part of Galatians 5:20.

Galatians 5:20

20 Idolatry, witchcraft, ... 152

Idolatry is putting anything before or in place of God. Witchcraft is controlling people, which is an attempt to replace the leading and guiding role of the Holy Spirit. Many times we can't produce our spiritual fruit because we are too busy putting other things in front of God. The pursuit of prosperity, jobs, homes, can make us too busy to do the will of God. Anything that takes precedent over the will of God is idolatry.

Others can have the production of their spiritual fruit inhibited by being a part of a group or a clique. Groups or cliques that form in many of our churches, for example, may have leaders that can direct the entire group to work against the leadership of the church, and thus against the will of God.

151*Holy Bible, New Living Translation,* (Wheaton, IL: Tyndale House Publishers, Inc.) 1996.
152*The King James Version,* (Cambridge: Cambridge) 1769.

Any form of control that works against the will of God is witchcraft.

Anti-Fruit: Sins Against Your Brother

Sins against your brother or sister are the third set of anti-fruit that inhibits the production of the fruit of the Spirit.

Galatians 5:20-21

20 ... hatred, variance, emulations, wrath, strife, seditions, heresies, 21 Envyings, murders, drunkenness, revellings, and such like: of the which I tell you before, as I have also told you in time past, that they which do such things shall not inherit the kingdom of God. 153

This third set of anti-fruit is one of the most important as it relates to our primary mission of winning others to Christ. It fights against the most important aspects of salvation itself, serving our fellowman. Before Jesus came and offered us salvation, we had the 10 commandments (Exodus 20). The abbreviated version is listed below:

1) Do not worship any other gods besides me.
2) Do not make idols of any kind, whether in the shape of birds or animals or fish.
3) Do not misuse the name of the Lord your God.
4) Remember to observe the Sabbath day by keeping it holy.
5) Honor your father and mother.
6) Do not murder.
7) Do not commit adultery.
8) Do not steal.

153*The King James Version*, (Cambridge: Cambridge) 1769.

9) Do not testify falsely against your neighbor.
10) Do not covet your neighbor's house, wife, or possessions.

However, we still couldn't produce good fruit, and because of our flesh, we kept on sinning. Paul said, "When I would do good, evil is present." As long as we are still dealing with the sins against our brothers and sisters, we will not be able to produce the fruit of love, joy, peace, longsuffering, gentleness, goodness, faith, meekness, and temperance.

Therefore, if we want good fruit of the Spirit produced in our lives, we have to kill off the anti-fruit. Think of anti-fruit as weeds that grow and prevent the real fruit from growing. We have to pull up the weeds so the good fruit can grow and flourish. We can't produce love if we allow hatred to run rampant in our heart. We can't show joy if we are always operating in jealousy. We can't demonstrate peace if there is discord and quarrels. We can't show gentleness if we are always involved in negative groups and cliques, and we can't produce goodness where there is always strife and envy.

Benefits from Producing the Fruit of the Spirit

When something has benefits, it generates interest, pays compensation, and comes with privileges and advantages. If you invest in something, you will want to know what is your rate of return. If you work for someone, you will want to know how much is your compensation. Joining certain organizations such as AAA will give you certain privileges and advantages. These things are known as benefits. There are also benefits associated with producing the fruit of the Spirit.

John 15:16

16 Ye have not chosen me, but I have chosen you, and ordained you, that ye should go and bring forth fruit, and that your fruit should remain: that whatsoever ye shall ask of the Father in my name, he may give it you. 154

First Things First

Everyone wants benefits! Many times before we will accept a job, we want to know what are the benefits. But "first things first"! Before one can obtain benefits, he must first meet the requirements. There are always prerequisites to benefits. You cannot obtain benefits from a company unless you first work for the company. You cannot gain interest on your money unless you deposit it into an interest-baring account. You cannot receive the privileges and advantages from AAA unless you first become a member.

154*The King James Version*, (Cambridge: Cambridge) 1769.

The fruit of the Holy Spirit gives us some of the greatest benefits we can ever hoped to obtain. We get a hundredfold blessing (1000 percent interest) according to Mark 4:20 on anything that we give up for God's sake. We get compensation that we will not have room enough to receive according to Malachi 3:10 when we give our tithes. We get advantages and privileges of being the head and not the tail according to Deuteronomy 28:13 when we obey the commandments of the lord.

Notice that each of these benefits had an associated requirement or prerequisite. Before we can reap the benefits that come from producing the fruit of the Holy Spirit, we must first meet the requirements.

John 15:7-8

7 If ye abide in me, and my words abide in you, ye shall ask what ye will, and it shall be done unto you. 8 Herein is my Father glorified, that ye bear much fruit; so shall ye be my disciples. 155

The benefit in this passage of scripture is very clear. Verse 7 says, "you shall ask what ye will, and it shall be done unto you". But first things first! The prerequisite is "if ye abide in me and my words abide in you". So what does it mean to abide in Christ? It means to abide in the Word of God for Christ is the Word. Verse 8 then says that as a result of abiding in Christ, God will be glorified because we will produce much fruit. These two verses are powerful; they say that the production of spiritual fruit has the benefit of giving us the ability to ask God for whatever we want, and because God is being glorified, he will do it for us. But all of this is

---

155*The King James Version*, (Cambridge: Cambridge) 1769.

assuming we meet the prerequisite or requirement of abiding in the Word of God.

The first Psalm teaches us what it means to abide in Christ or abide in the Word of God.

Psalm 1:1-3

Blessed is the man that walketh not in the counsel of the ungodly, nor standeth in the way of sinners, nor sitteth in the seat of the scornful. 2 But his delight is in the law of the LORD; and in his law doth he meditate day and night. 3 And he shall be like a tree planted by the rivers of water, that bringeth forth his fruit in his season; his leaf also shall not wither; and whatsoever he doeth shall prosper. 156

Verse 2 says we should meditate on the law or Word of God day and night. So abiding in Christ is meditating on the Word of God, allowing it to become a part of our heart. The more we meditate on the Word of God, the more we become like Christ. And when people see us, they will see Christ because we will be producing fruit of the Holy Spirit. We will then be able to take advantages of his benefits.

Our ability to produce the fruit of the Spirit is related directly to the place the Word of God has in our lives; and thus determines our benefits package. The longer you work for a company (demonstrating commitment), the more your benefits package will increase. You may get more vacation, more medical, or more retirement moneys. Well the more we mediate on God's Word, the more we will produce fruit of the Spirit, and thus the more our Spiritual benefits package will increase. As we become more and more like Christ, we will

---

156*The King James Version*, (Cambridge: Cambridge) 1769.

reap the same benefits he reaped while on earth. As a result of the Spirit of God, we receive the basic benefits:

We get medical benefits:

Isaiah 53:5

5 But he was wounded for our transgressions, he was bruised for our iniquities: the chastisement of our peace was upon him; and with his stripes we are healed. 157

We get legal attorney or advocate benefits:

1 John 2:1

My little children, these things write I unto you, that ye sin not. And if any man sin, we have an advocate with the Father, Jesus Christ the righteous: 158

We get financial benefits:

Deuteronomy 28:2

2 And all these blessings shall come on thee, and overtake thee, if thou shalt hearken unto the voice of the LORD thy God. 159

We get companionship benefits:

Hebrews 13:5

157*The King James Version*, (Cambridge: Cambridge) 1769.
158*The King James Version*, (Cambridge: Cambridge) 1769.
159*The King James Version*, (Cambridge: Cambridge) 1769.

5 Let your conversation be without covetousness; and be content with such things as ye have: for he hath said, I will never leave thee, nor forsake thee. 160

We get emotional benefits:

Philippians 4:7

7 And the peace of God, which passeth all understanding, shall keep your hearts and minds through Christ Jesus. 161

But perhaps the greatest benefit that we receive is found in John 15:7. Simply put, we have the benefit of asking God for whatever we will, and he will do it. Verse 16 explains it more:

John 15:16

16 Ye have not chosen me, but I have chosen you, and ordained you, that ye should go and bring forth fruit, and that your fruit should remain: that whatsoever ye shall ask of the Father in my name, he may give it you. 162

Notice the further qualification on this benefit. It is "In My Name"! It means that we must ask according to his name, and we must use his name.

Benefits According to the Name of Jesus

James 4:3

160*The King James Version*, (Cambridge: Cambridge) 1769.
161*The King James Version*, (Cambridge: Cambridge) 1769.
162*The King James Version*, (Cambridge: Cambridge) 1769.

3 Ye ask, and receive not, because ye ask amiss, that ye may consume it upon your lusts. 163

James 4:3

3 And even when you do ask, you don't get it because your whole motive is wrong—you want only what will give you pleasure. 164

The benefit of asking God for whatever we want must be according to his will. The request that we place to God must not have the wrong motives. I have seen bracelets with the acronym "WWJD". It means "What Would Jesus Do"! To make sure our petitions to God are not with the wrong motives, we must think "WWJD". How do we get to the point where our petitions line up with the will of God? We have to meditate on the Word of God. We begin to think like him, act like him, and request the things that he would request in our situation.

Benefits in the Name of Jesus

Perhaps you have heard of the phrase "I got the hook-up"! It simply means that you received some benefit as a result of who you knew. If I owned a bank and you were my friend, you would have the hook-up if I sent you to the loan officer and told you to tell him "Wil Nichols, the owner of the bank sent me". You would be there in my name and would be treated as if I was there myself.

When we pray and say "in the name of Jesus", we are coming to God saying Jesus sent us. When we rebuke the

---

163*The King James Version*, (Cambridge: Cambridge) 1769.
164*Holy Bible, New Living Translation*, (Wheaton, IL: Tyndale House Publishers, Inc.) 1996.

devil, we are telling him Jesus sent us. It is as if Jesus himself is praying our prayer for us. When we need anything from God, we can simply go to him and say, "Jesus sent me".

John 14:6

6 Jesus told him, "I am the way, the truth, and the life. No one can come to the Father except through me. 165

165*Holy Bible, New Living Translation*, (Wheaton, IL: Tyndale House Publishers, Inc.) 1996.

The Three Clusters of the Fruit of the Spirit

Now let us look at the elements that make up the fruit of the Spirit. If you recall from the chapter on anti-fruit, the works of the flesh are divided into three groups or categories; sins against the body (fornication, lusts), sins against God (idolatry, witchcraft), and sins against your brother (hatred, envy, wrath). Well the fruit of the Sprit can be divided into three groups or categories as well; however they deal with relationships as opposed to sin!

Galatians 5:22-23

22 But the fruit of the Spirit is love, joy, peace, longsuffering, gentleness, goodness, faith, 23 Meekness, temperance: against such there is no law. 166

There are nine elements of the fruit of the Spirit. They are subdivided into your relationship with God (Love, Joy, Peace), your relationship with your Brother (Longsuffering/Patience, Gentleness/Kindness, Goodness), and your relationship within yourself (Faith/Faithfulness, Meekness, Temperance/Self-control).

Love

Many of us perhaps have a memory about our first love. Maybe it was a good experience, and maybe it was not. For some people, their first love was all they wanted in a mate and they ended up marrying them. But for others, their first love turned out to be a jerk. Either their love was not reciprocated or their heart was broken through unfaithfulness.

166*The King James Version*, (Cambridge: Cambridge) 1769.

A songwriter wrote a song titled "All we need is a little more love". Another songwriter wrote a song titled "What's love got to do with it". One writer says, "With a little more love we can work it out". And yet another one says, "Who needs a heart when a heart can be broken".

Why such polar opposites? In our society we see one couple happily married for 50 years, while another couple is involved in constant domestic abuse. Both couples claim they have love, so what's the difference? It can be found in the fruit of the Spirit.

Most of us know love as a human emotion. This type of love typically works best when it is reciprocal. When a man loves a woman, he needs her to love him back. When one of them feels that the love is not being reciprocated, problems will develop. However, the love that's listed as one of the fruit of the Spirit is not this human emotional love, but is a divinely given love from God called "agape" love. It is why the love associated with the fruit of the Spirit is about our relationship with God and not about our relationship with our brother.

Matthew 5:44

44 But I say unto you, Love your enemies, bless them that curse you, do good to them that hate you, and pray for them which despitefully use you, and persecute you; 167

As you can see from this commandment of Jesus, human emotions will not work here. Emotional love requires reciprocation; it requires those that we love to love us back. However Jesus tells us to love those that hate us. From a

---

167*The King James Version*, (Cambridge: Cambridge) 1769.

human perspective, this is not possible. This type of love can only come from God and has nothing to do with human emotion.

John 3:16

16 For God so loved the world, that he gave his only begotten Son, that whosoever believeth in him should not perish, but have everlasting life. 168

Notice that God loved us without any requirement of us loving him back. This kind of love comes directly from God!

1 John 4:8

8 He that loveth not knoweth not God; for God is love. 169

God loves us because he is love and he can't help but love. Even when we were sinners he loved us because he was love. So in order for us to obey the commandment of Jesus to love our enemies, we need to develop the spiritual fruit of love in our lives. This type of love, agape love, is developed in us through the Holy Spirit.

When an apple grows, all it knows is how to be an apple, nothing else. When the fruit of the spirit grows and matures in us, all it knows is how to be fruit. When agape love is produced in us, all it knows is how to love, even if the person is our enemy.

John 13:35

168*The King James Version*, (Cambridge: Cambridge) 1769.
169*The King James Version*, (Cambridge: Cambridge) 1769.

35 By this shall all men know that ye are my disciples, if ye have love one to another. 170

1 John 3:14

14 We know that we have passed from death unto life, because we love the brethren. He that loveth not his brother abideth in death. 171

1 John 3:14

14 If we love our Christian brothers and sisters, it proves that we have passed from death to eternal life. But a person who has no love is still dead. 172

From a religious perspective, we are in a gift-dominated culture. We become drawn to churches, preachers, teachers, prophets, healers, and miracle workers because of their gifts. But generally we may never know what their fruit production capabilities are. As Christians we can become excited and drawn to gifts, but it is the fruit that is really going to make the difference in our ability to complete our mission.

1 Corinthians 13:1-3

1 If I could speak in any language in heaven or on earth but didn't love others, I would only be making meaningless noise like a loud gong or a clanging cymbal. 2 If I had the gift of prophecy, and if I knew all the mysteries of the future and knew everything about everything, but didn't love others, what good would I be? And if I had the gift of faith so

170*The King James Version*, (Cambridge: Cambridge) 1769.
171*The King James Version*, (Cambridge: Cambridge) 1769.
172*Holy Bible, New Living Translation*, (Wheaton, IL: Tyndale House Publishers, Inc.) 1996.

that I could speak to a mountain and make it move, without love I would be no good to anybody. 3 If I gave everything I have to the poor and even sacrificed my body, I could boast about it; but if I didn't love others, I would be of no value whatsoever. 173

Love is to the heart as summer is to the farmer. It brings about the harvest. No summer, no harvest! No love, no harvest! Many of us have not reaped the harvest of God's blessings because we have not produced his fruit of love.

God's love is what fulfills us! Without it we are empty. When man sinned, we lost our direct relationship with God. That relationship had love in it because God is love. The commandments that were given to us from Moses were intended to bridge the gap, but man could not keep them. And so Jesus came to fulfill what the law could not do.

Matthew 5:17

17 Think not that I am come to destroy the law, or the prophets: I am not come to destroy, but to fulfil. 174

And how did Jesus fulfill the law given to Moses? With one commandment!

John 13:34

34 A new commandment I give unto you, That ye love one another; as I have loved you, that ye also love one another. 175

173*Holy Bible, New Living Translation,* (Wheaton, IL: Tyndale House Publishers, Inc.) 1996.
174*The King James Version,* (Cambridge: Cambridge) 1769.
175*The King James Version,* (Cambridge: Cambridge) 1769.

Romans 13:8

8 Owe no man any thing, but to love one another: for he that loveth another hath fulfilled the law. 176

Why should we place such an emphasis on the fruit of the Spirit and on God's love? Because the Holy Bible teaches us to do so!

1 Peter 4:8

8 Most important of all, continue to show deep love for each other, for love covers a multitude of sins. 177

Let us now look more into the differences between God's love and human emotional love. God's love, translated in the Hebrew is "agape" love, and means charity, brotherly love, affection, good will, benevolence, compassion, and grace. This particular love is only found in the New Testament of the Holy Bible. The love that is found in the Old Testament of the Holy Bible is translated "oahab", and means friends, beloved, family love, or sexual love. It is what I call human emotional love.

This distinction of "agape" love and "oahab" love is very interesting. "Oahab" love was in the Old Testament, which is where we also see laws to deal with our enemies such as "an eye for an eye". In other words, the Old Testament taught us that if our enemy hit us, we should hit him back.

Exodus 21:23-24

176*The King James Version*, (Cambridge: Cambridge) 1769.
177*Holy Bible, New Living Translation*, (Wheaton, IL: Tyndale House Publishers, Inc.) 1996.

23 And if any mischief follow, then thou shalt give life for life, 24 Eye for eye, tooth for tooth, hand for hand, foot for foot, 178

Simply put, we were to pay our enemies back according to how they hurt us! But in the New Testament, Jesus gave us a different commandment concerning the treatment of our enemies.

Matthew 5:38-39

38 Ye have heard that it hath been said, An eye for an eye, and a tooth for a tooth: 39 But I say unto you, That ye resist not evil: but whosoever shall smite thee on thy right cheek, turn to him the other also. 179

Matthew 5:43-44

43 Ye have heard that it hath been said, Thou shalt love thy neighbour, and hate thine enemy. 44 But I say unto you, Love your enemies, bless them that curse you, do good to them that hate you, and pray for them which despitefully use you, and persecute you; 180

Jesus was not saying it would be nice if we had "agape" love, he was requiring us to have it. Jesus saved the world with this type of love, and as his disciples, we are required to have it. Our job is not to win just our friends and loved ones, but even our enemies. As Christians, we will not win the lost because we are a gifted church, a strong church, a big church, a rich church, a hot church, or even an "on-fire" church; but we will win the lost because we are a loving church.

178*The King James Version*, (Cambridge: Cambridge) 1769.
179*The King James Version*, (Cambridge: Cambridge) 1769.
180*The King James Version*, (Cambridge: Cambridge) 1769.

Joy

When it comes to understanding what joy is, we must first understand what it is not! Most people think of joy as happiness, but true joy is an element of the fruit of the Spirit, and happiness is not.

People are happy when things are going well in their lives. The wedding day or birth of a child can bring some people happiness. Others become happy when they get a new job, a substantial bonus, or an unexpected financial increase. Happiness is a good thing, but it has a flaw. It is contingent upon the circumstances in one's life. In the circumstances described earlier, they produced happiness. But when life enters into the times of despair, loss, rejection, or even death, happiness departs. A friend of mine sent me the following email concerning joy versus happiness:

"Joy has its secret within itself, untouchable and completely independent of all the chances and circumstances of life. However the root word of happiness is "hap", which means chance. Happiness is completely dependant on life's chances. True joy is a permanent joy that nothing can take away."

Even as happiness flees when life's circumstances take a downward turn, the joy that comes from the Holy Spirit will shine through.

Psalm 30:5

5 For his anger endureth but a moment; in his favour is life: weeping may endure for a night, but joy cometh in the morning. 181

Another friend shared this story with me concerning inner joy in times of life's tough circumstances:

"A Pastor went to the Hospital to visit one of his female members who had just had her third amputation. He walked into the room expected to see her depressed, but instead found her in good spirits. And as he thought about what he would say to console her, she looked up and said to him, Pastor, I always knew I was going to go to heaven, I just didn't know it would be one piece at a time."

This woman clearly had inner joy that allowed her to have humor during a very tough time in her life. But for the most part, most people do not have this joy. They do not have the joy of the Lord that brings strength during times of trouble. Many people are looking for it, but they are looking in all the wrong places.

Some people think that if they can just get married, then they will be happy. While others think they will be happy if they can get a divorce. People out of work feel that they will achieve happiness if they can just get a good paying job. Yet others are frustrated with the jobs they have and can't wait to be able to quit. People become workaholics, womanizers, shop-aholics, and more, all in an attempt to obtain sustainable happiness. They move from relationship to relationship, from job to job, from church to church looking for a lasting happiness. The problem is that the things they are looking to are not sustainable.

---

181 *The King James Version*, (Cambridge: Cambridge) 1769.

Ecclesiastes 3:1-8

To every thing there is a season, and a time to every purpose under the heaven: 2 A time to be born, and a time to die; a time to plant, and a time to pluck up that which is planted; 3 A time to kill, and a time to heal; a time to break down, and a time to build up; 4 A time to weep, and a time to laugh; a time to mourn, and a time to dance; 5 A time to cast away stones, and a time to gather stones together; a time to embrace, and a time to refrain from embracing; 6 A time to get, and a time to lose; a time to keep, and a time to cast away; 7 A time to rend, and a time to sew; a time to keep silence, and a time to speak; 8 A time to love, and a time to hate; a time of war, and a time of peace. 182

According to this passage, if you give things enough time they will change. Everything that we seek after for happiness will eventually change over time. People will change, attitudes will change, jobs will change, finances will change, and circumstances will change because there is a time and a season for everything. So the answer is to stop seeking after things to bring happiness, but seek after the Lord who can bring true joy that will never change. It will never change because God will never change.

Malachi 3:6

6 For I am the LORD, I change not; therefore ye sons of Jacob are not consumed. 183

True joy, that is a part of the fruit of the Spirit, is not affected by the ups and downs of life. It is not affected by the cares of life because it does not come from the chances of life; it comes from God.

182*The King James Version*, (Cambridge: Cambridge) 1769.
183*The King James Version*, (Cambridge: Cambridge) 1769.

1 Thessalonians 1:6-7

6 So you received the message with joy from the Holy Spirit in spite of the severe suffering it brought you. In this way, you imitated both us and the Lord. 7 As a result, you yourselves became an example to all the Christians in Greece. 184

This is a powerful passage. It first shows how the joy of the Lord remains with us in spite of severe suffering. Secondly, it brings out the purpose of the fruit of the Spirit, which is to make us like Christ for an example to the world. When the Holy Spirit produces the joy of the Lord in us during times of suffering, we become examples to other Christians as a source of encouragement. We also become examples to the unsaved, demonstrating the power of the Holy Spirit during these tough times, and thus draw them to Christ.

Not only does God's spiritual joy remain with us in times of trouble and suffering, it also gives us strength to take us through these times. The early Christian church was severely persecuted. The Christians of these times were hunted like dogs, whipped and beaten, boiled in hot oil, stoned to death, thrown to hungry lions, and crucified upside down on crosses. But somehow, they still had joy.

2 Corinthians 4:8-9

8 We are troubled on every side, yet not distressed; we are perplexed, but not in despair; 9 Persecuted, but not forsaken; cast down, but not destroyed; 185

184*Holy Bible, New Living Translation*, (Wheaton, IL: Tyndale House Publishers, Inc.) 1996.
185*The King James Version*, (Cambridge: Cambridge) 1769.

Nehemiah 8:10

10 Then he said unto them, Go your way, eat the fat, and drink the sweet, and send portions unto them for whom nothing is prepared: for this day is holy unto our Lord: neither be ye sorry; for the joy of the LORD is your strength. 186

Nehemiah says the joy of the Lord is our strength. So if a person does not allow the Holy Spirit to grow fruit in them, he or she will miss out on a source of strength. And when you are weak, life's troubles will get the best of you. However, when you have joy, you can respond to trouble in an entirely different manner. James said, whenever trouble comes your way, let it be an opportunity to put your joy into action:

James 1:2-3

2 Dear brothers and sisters, whenever trouble comes your way, let it be an opportunity for joy. 3 For when your faith is tested, your endurance has a chance to grow. 187

Peace

Just as there is human love versus spiritual love, human joy versus spiritual joy, there is also human peace versus spiritual peace. And as it is with love and joy, we must allow the Holy Spirit to produce spiritual peace in us.

From a human perspective, we think of peace as a state of national tranquility, exemption from war, or peace between individuals. It is harmony, concord, security, safety, or

---

186*The King James Version*, (Cambridge: Cambridge) 1769.
187*Holy Bible, New Living Translation*, (Wheaton, IL: Tyndale House Publishers, Inc.) 1996.

prosperity. This type of peace is conveyed by the absence of discord, confusion, or noise.

On the other hand, the peace that is produced from the Holy Spirit is translated in the Hebrew language as the tranquil state of a soul assured of its salvation through Christ, and so fearing nothing, content with its earthly lot. And so as Christians, we must understand this difference so that we seek after the right type of peace.

At Christmas, we always hear the phrase, "Peace on earth, goodwill towards all men". The theme of this phrase is an attitude that we have come to associate with being a Christian. It is a mythical state of peace where there is no confusion, no discord, no fighting; a place where everyone just gets along with everyone else. I've heard of people leaving the church choir or even the church altogether because they felt that there was too much confusion or infighting. People will leave jobs, neighborhoods, organizations, friends, and spouses in an attempt to get away from hostility and find peace.   Christians have justified this attitude from the following passage:

1 Corinthians 14:33

33 For God is not the author of confusion, but of peace, as in all churches of the saints. 188

So we may conclude that Christ came with the same message as Rodney King, "Can't We All Just Get Along?". But this conclusion would be incorrect. Let's study the 10th chapter of Matthew when Jesus sent his disciples to preach the Gospel of Peace.

188*The King James Version*, (Cambridge: Cambridge) 1769.

Matthew 10:5-7

5 These twelve Jesus sent forth, and commanded them, saying, Go not into the way of the Gentiles, and into any city of the Samaritans enter ye not: 6 But go rather to the lost sheep of the house of Israel. 7 And as ye go, preach, saying, The kingdom of heaven is at hand. 189

Now from the 5th verse through the 15th verse, Jesus gives instructions on how the disciples should conduct themselves while preaching the gospel. But when we get to the 16th verse, he tells them what the environment will be like.

Matthew 10:16-17

16 Behold, I send you forth as sheep in the midst of wolves: be ye therefore wise as serpents, and harmless as doves. 17 But beware of men: for they will deliver you up to the councils, and they will scourge you in their synagogues; 190

Jesus was telling them that preaching the Gospel of Peace would not be a peaceful mission. There would be people trying to kill and destroy them. And when we get to the 34th verse, Jesus clearly states that our concept of peace was not what his mission was all about:

Matthew 10:34-35

34 "Don't imagine that I came to bring peace to the earth! No, I came to bring a sword. 35 I have come to set a

---

189*The King James Version*, (Cambridge: Cambridge) 1769.
190*The King James Version*, (Cambridge: Cambridge) 1769.

*man against his father. and a daughter against her mother,
and a daughter-in-law against her mother-in-law. 191*

To preach the Gospel of Peace is actually a declaration
of war. Look at what Jesus said in the 11th chapter of
Matthew:

Matthew 11:12

*12 And from the time John the Baptist began preaching
and baptizing until now. the Kingdom of Heaven has been
forcefully advancing, and violent people attack it. 192*

Jesus declared in this passage that the mission of the
church would not be one of peace, but one of war. And even
Paul told us to be prepared for this war in his letter to the
Ephesians:

Ephesians 6:10-12

*10 Finally, let the mighty strength of the Lord make
you strong. 11 Put on all the armor that God gives, so you can
defend yourself against the devil's tricks. 12 We are not
fighting against humans. We are fighting against forces and
authorities and against rulers of darkness and powers in the
spiritual world. 193*

The reason Jesus did NOT come to bring the world the
tranquil, harmonious peace that we many times seek as

191*Holy Bible, New Living Translation*, (Wheaton, IL:
Tyndale House Publishers, Inc.) 1996.
192*Holy Bible, New Living Translation*, (Wheaton, IL:
Tyndale House Publishers, Inc.) 1996.
193*The Contemporary English [computer file], electronic ed.,
Logos Library System*, (Nashville: Thomas Nelson) 1997,
c1995 by the American Bible Society.

Christians is because we are at war. The Holy Bible says in John 10:10, the thief comes to kill, steal, and destroy. Satan is trying to kill us. He wants to destroy our homes, our families, our jobs, our finances, and our churches. He wants to destroy our very way of life. You can't be at peace with someone who is trying to kill you!

Now as a Christian, if you are trying to "just get along" with everyone, you are never going to find that type of peace here on earth. We have to stop going from church to church, from relationship to relationship, from friend to friend, and from spouse to spouse trying to find peace. This is not the type of peace Jesus came to bring, and it is not the type of peace that the Holy Spirit will produce.

So let's look to Paul to understand this spiritual peace that comes from God:

Romans 8:5-7

5 For they that are after the flesh do mind the things of the flesh; but they that are after the Spirit the things of the Spirit. 6 For to be carnally minded is death; but to be spiritually minded is life and peace. 7 Because the carnal mind is enmity against God: for it is not subject to the law of God, neither indeed can be. 194

Verse 7 says that to be carnally minded (controlled by our sinful nature) is to be at enmity against God. Enmity means to be in a state of hostility or at war. This is the state that all men entered into when man (Adam) sinned in the Garden of Eden. But when you look at verse 6, it says that to be spiritually minded is life and peace. This is to say that the

---

194*The King James Version*, (Cambridge: Cambridge) 1769.

state of hostility or war has ended, and we are now at peace with God.

The next set of passages then explains how this peace benefits us as Christians who are allowing the Holy Spirit to produce its fruit in us.

Philippians 4:6-7

6 Be careful for nothing; but in every thing by prayer and supplication with thanksgiving let your requests be made known unto God. 7 And the peace of God, which passeth all understanding, shall keep your hearts and minds through Christ Jesus. 195

Most people when they have trouble enter into a state of worry. But this passage says that Christians shouldn't worry about anything because they have the peace of God to keep them. Since we are at peace with God, we can go to him in prayer with our trouble, and he will give us a peace that non-Christians can't understand.

The power of this spiritual peace is that when everyone else is losing their head, our minds will be kept in perfect peace. God doesn't necessarily put us at peace with our adversaries, nor does he necessarily fix our troubling situations, he simply produces a spiritual peace so strong that the adversaries or situations no longer matter. Study the next two passages:

Isaiah 26:3

195*The King James Version*, (Cambridge: Cambridge) 1769.

3 Thou wilt keep him in perfect peace, whose mind is stayed on thee: because he trusteth in thee. 196

John 14:27

27 Peace I leave with you, my peace I give unto you: not as the world giveth, give I unto you. Let not your heart be troubled, neither let it be afraid. 197;

Let me restate the definition of spiritual peace: it is the tranquil state of a soul assured of its salvation through Christ, and so fearing nothing, content with its earthly lot. This peace brings God and man back together and places in man an inner peace beyond understanding. It comes from God and is produced in us by the Holy Spirit.

Longsuffering, Gentleness, and Goodness

Love, joy, and peace were what I call the first cluster of the fruit of Spirit. They were divided into the first cluster because they represented our relationship with God. We learned that we should not look to people to fulfill our needs for love, joy, and peace, but we should look to God. We will often refer to this cluster of fruit in Godly terms: "The Love of God", "The Joy of the Lord", and "The Gospel of Peace".

When people are not demonstrating love, joy, or peace, their relationship with God has become affected. They may say that no one loves them, that life has them depressed, or that there's no one that brings joy to their life. But they are wrong, because these things must first come from the Lord.

196*The King James Version*, (Cambridge: Cambridge) 1769.
197*The King James Version*, (Cambridge: Cambridge) 1769.

Now after we get our relationship together with God, the next cluster of the fruit of the Spirit will helps us with our relationship with our brothers. This cluster of fruit is longsuffering, gentleness, and goodness.

Longsuffering, gentleness, and goodness is the cluster of spiritual fruit that help us to get along with each other. When you see people who are always fighting, arguing, impatient, mean, or unkind, then you are dealing with people who are not producing the second cluster of fruit. Let us look at each of the elements of this cluster.

Longsuffering is patience, endurance, constancy, steadfastness, perseverance. It is steadfastness under provocation, patiently enduring ill treatment without anger or thought of retaliation or revenge. And so this part of the fruit of the Spirit is seen in our relationship with our neighbor.

If we are irritable, vengeful, resentful, and malicious to our neighbors, then we are short suffering and not long-suffering, and the Holy Spirit is not producing fruit.

Longsuffering or patience is a loving and tender heart that deals kindly and graciously with the people around it. It deals with the faults of others without criticism. The reason why we can't get along with others many times is because we have no longsuffering or patience with our brothers.

Matthew 18:21-22

21 Then Peter came to him and asked, "Lord, how often should I forgive someone who sins against me? Seven times?" 22 "No!" Jesus replied, "seventy times seven! 198

198*Holy Bible, New Living Translation*, (Wheaton, IL: Tyndale House Publishers, Inc.) 1996.

Jesus said we should forgive our brother 490 times per offence. It isn't the literal number that's important here, but the fact that we should continue to forgive each other without concern for how many times they have wronged.

Longsuffering is closely related to testing when we study the book of James:

James 1:2-4

2 Dear brothers and sisters, whenever trouble comes your way, let it be an opportunity for joy. 3 For when your faith is tested, your endurance has a chance to grow. 4 So let it grow, for when your endurance is fully developed, you will be strong in character and ready for anything. 199

Many times we may show patience in good times, but how do we react when trials come. It is this time when our longsuffering fruit needs to kick in.

When a person eats fruit, the fruit provides vitamins such as vitamin A, B, C, Zinc, and Calcium. These vitamins protect the body against diseases such as rickets and osteoporosis. These diseases cause compression of the vertebrae, back pain, bone fractures, painful muscular contraction, convulsions, and bleeding to death. A person should be happy to eat their fruit if they know it's going to prevent these types of diseases from attacking their body.

So James is teaching us that we should be happy when we have trials, because the trials then produce patience or longsuffering. Longsuffering is one of our spiritual vitamins

---

199*Holy Bible, New Living Translation*, (Wheaton, IL: Tyndale House Publishers, Inc.) 1996.

that protect us against spiritual diseases. In this case, the spiritual diseases are the things that get in the way of our relationship with our brothers.

The next element of the second cluster of the fruit of the Spirit is gentleness. Gentleness is kindness, compassion, benevolence, mercy, and tenderness. Jesus came to bring us gentleness, kindness, and mercy.

Prior to the coming of Jesus, there were few institutions of mercy, few hospitals, few mental institutions, or places of refuge for the poor. But Jesus changed all that.

Luke 4:18

18 The Spirit of the Lord is upon me, because he hath anointed me to preach the gospel to the poor; he hath sent me to heal the brokenhearted, to preach deliverance to the captives, and recovering of sight to the blind, to set at liberty them that are bruised. 200

The people that Jesus came for were the poor, brokenhearted, captives, blind, and bruised. These were people who could not help themselves. Clearly they had nothing to offer Jesus, so he came because of his gentleness or compassion.

Jeremiah 31:3

3 The LORD hath appeared of old unto me, saying, Yea, I have loved thee with an everlasting love: therefore with lovingkindness have I drawn thee. 201

200*The King James Version*, (Cambridge: Cambridge) 1769.
201*The King James Version*, (Cambridge: Cambridge) 1769.

We were drawn to God through gentleness, and it is the same gentleness we must use towards each other. In our contempt for sin, we cannot be harsh or unkind to sinners. Many sinners on the verge of redemption have been disillusioned by the coldness and harshness of Christians hung up on legalistic religious codes. But Jesus had a gentleness about him that caused even little children to approach him.

2 Timothy 2:24

24 The Lord's servants must not quarrel but must be kind to everyone. They must be able to teach effectively and be patient with difficult people. 202

Some people may believe that gentleness is a sign of weakness. Abraham Lincoln was well known for his gentleness. But it can never be said that he was weak. We must never mistake gentleness for weakness. Gentleness is about strength of character with a compassionate spirit.

The last element of the second cluster of the fruit of the Spirit is goodness. Goodness is that quality found in a person who is ruled by what is good and represents the highest moral and ethical values.

Ephesians 5:9

9 (For the fruit of the Spirit is in all goodness and righteousness and truth;) 203

Romans 15:14

202*Holy Bible, New Living Translation*, (Wheaton, IL: Tyndale House Publishers, Inc.) 1996.
203*The King James Version*, (Cambridge: Cambridge) 1769.

14 And I myself also am persuaded of you, my brethren, that ye also are full of goodness, filled with all knowledge, able also to admonish one another. 204

Just as a clean and pure spring produces the purest water, a good heart always produces goodness. Goodness means to be like God, because God is perfectly good. It is one thing to have high ethical standards, but it's another to have the Holy Spirit that produces goodness.

This goodness comes from the depth of God. It's deeper than just doing good deeds. It's doing good to please God without expectation of reward. Although some people may by nature be good; the goodness from the Holy Spirit will change a mean and evil person into goodness.

These first two clusters of fruit can be summed up in the 23rd Psalm.

Psalm 23:1-6

1 The LORD is my shepherd; I shall not want. (LOVE OF GOD) 2 He maketh me to lie down in green pastures: he leadeth me beside the still waters. (JOY OF THE LORD) 3 He restoreth my soul: he leadeth me in the paths of righteousness for his name's sake. (PEACE OF GOD) 4 Yea, though I walk through the valley of the shadow of death, I will fear no evil: for thou art with me; thy rod and thy staff they comfort me. (LONGSUFFERING) 5 Thou preparest a table before me in the presence of mine enemies: thou anointest my head with oil; my cup runneth over. 6 Surely goodness and mercy shall follow me all the days of my life: and I will dwell

---

204*The King James Version*, (Cambridge: Cambridge) 1769.

in the house of the LORD forever. (GOODNESS & GENTLENESS) *205*

Faith, Meekness, Temperance

The third cluster of fruit of the Spirit is faith, meekness, and temperance. This cluster deals with our internal relationship with ourselves. God doesn't do anything by mistake, so it is not a coincidence that the clusters of the fruit of the Spirit are given in the order that we see them in the book of Galatians.

Galatians 5:22-23

22 But the fruit of the Spirit is love, joy, peace, longsuffering, gentleness, goodness, faith, 23 Meekness, temperance: against such there is no law. 206

Just to review; love, joy, and peace make up the first cluster of fruit that deals with our relationship with God. Longsuffering, gentleness, and goodness make up the second cluster of fruit that deals with our relationship with our fellowman. Faith, meekness, and temperance make up the third and last cluster of fruit that deals with our relationship with self or ourselves. This order therefore lets us know that our relationships should be ordered as God first, our fellowman second, and ourselves last.

Luke 9:23

23 And he said to them all, If any man will come after me, let him deny himself, and take up his cross daily, and follow me. 207

205*The King James Version*, (Cambridge: Cambridge) 1769.
206*The King James Version*, (Cambridge: Cambridge) 1769.

When people say "I've got to get myself together before I can give my life to God", or say "I've got to deal with myself before I can deal with other people", they are actually out of order. The priority of our lives must always be God first, others second, and self last.

So now we look at the third and last cluster of fruit, faith, meekness, and temperance.

Philippians 2:13

13 For it is God which worketh in you both to will and to do of his good pleasure. 208

Philippians 2:13

13 For God is working in you, giving you the desire to obey him and the power to do what pleases him. 209

When dealing with self, we must first understand that this relationship is not about us or our will, but about God and his will. The scripture here says God works both the "Will" and the "Do". Will is desires, and Do is Power.

The Holy Spirit dwelling within us makes abundant life a reality, not just a possibility. But again it's not about us.

Matthew 16:24-27

24 Then said Jesus unto his disciples, If any man will come after me, let him deny himself, and take up his cross, and

---

207*The King James Version*, (Cambridge: Cambridge) 1769.
208*The King James Version*, (Cambridge: Cambridge) 1769.
209*Holy Bible, New Living Translation*, (Wheaton, IL: Tyndale House Publishers, Inc.) 1996.

follow me. 25 For whosoever will save his life shall lose it: and whosoever will lose his life for my sake shall find it. 26 For what is a man profited, if he shall gain the whole world, and lose his own soul? or what shall a man give in exchange for his soul? 27 For the Son of man shall come in the glory of his Father with his angels; and then he shall reward every man according to his works. 210

The first element of this last cluster of fruit is faith. This faith, however, is not faith in the sense of believing or having faith in God. That faith, which we are all commanded to have in order to please God, is simply a belief in the Word of God, and in Jesus as the Messiah. However, the faith referred to in Galatians as part of the fruit of the Spirit is actually translated "faithfulness". It means fidelity, the character of one who can be relied on; and this kind of faith (faithfulness) is produced by the Holy Spirit.

Perhaps you know of someone that you cannot rely or depend upon. The problem is that they are missing fruit! As a Pastor, I've learned to NOT depend on the words of people who say, "I'm with you pastor". I just sit back and wait to see the fruit. Those that allow this fruit to flourish in their lives can be epitomized by the phrase "swear to his own hurt and change not"!

Titus 2:9-10

9 Exhort servants to be obedient unto their own masters, and to please them well in all things; not answering again; 10 Not purloining, but shewing all good fidelity; that they may adorn the doctrine of God our Saviour in all things. 211

210*The King James Version*, (Cambridge: Cambridge) 1769.
211*The King James Version*, (Cambridge: Cambridge) 1769.

If we do not possess faithfulness, we will be missing one of the elements necessary to complete our primary mission, winning others to Christ. If we borrow money and are not faithful in paying it back, if we have a job and are not faithful in doing an honest days work, how are we going to win those we interact with to Christ?

God takes a very dim view of an unfaithful person:

Matthew 25:29-30

29 To those who use well what they are given, even more will be given, and they will have an abundance. But from those who are unfaithful, even what little they have will be taken away. 30 Now throw this useless servant into outer darkness, where there will be weeping and gnashing of teeth.
212

Regardless of who we are or what we have, God wants us to be faithful in it. Don't wait until you get a better job to become a faithful tither or giver. Don't wait until you get married to become a faithful worker in the church. God wants us to be faithful, and the Holy Spirit is given to us to produce this fruit.

This second element of this cluster of fruit is meekness.

Matthew 5:5

5 Blessed are the meek: for they shall inherit the earth.
213

212*Holy Bible, New Living Translation*, (Wheaton, IL: Tyndale House Publishers, Inc.) 1996.
213*The King James Version*, (Cambridge: Cambridge) 1769.

Philippians 2:5-8

5 Let this mind be in you, which was also in Christ Jesus: 6 Who, being in the form of God, thought it not robbery to be equal with God: 7 But made himself of no reputation, and took upon him the form of a servant, and was made in the likeness of men: 8 And being found in fashion as a man, he humbled himself, and became obedient unto death, even the death of the cross. 214

Meekness has nothing to do with being timid. Jesus was far from timid. He took on the religious establishment, he stood up against corruption in the temple of God, and he accepted persecution although he had the power to destroy the world.

Meekness is controlled or disciplined power. A wild horse that has been tamed is still powerful; it simply has learned how to control its power. Controlled power is how one gets the power to accomplish a specific purpose. A wild river under control can generate power for an entire city; a fire under control can be used to heat a home.

When we display meekness, we are not being weak; we are simply controlling our power to be used for God's purpose. Peter, James, and John, three of Jesus' disciples were very strong men. Peter was a fighter, and James and John were called the sons of thunder. These were "rough-neck" strong men of their times. But Jesus taught them meekness so they could be the first apostles! He needed their power to establish the first church.

214*The King James Version*, (Cambridge: Cambridge) 1769.

God wants to take our strength and energy and use it for his purpose. But this will only happen if we have meekness.

Meekness is the opposite of a flamboyant and self-indulgent spirit. It displays a sensitive regard for others. Jesus throughout his trial, torture, and crucifixion endured the emotional and physical pain without ever opening his mouth, or using his power against his tormentors. Like a sheep being led to the slaughter, he remained silent trusting instead in God. Unlike pride which comes from looking at ourselves, our strength, and our abilities; meekness comes from looking at God, his strength, and his abilities.

Meekness teaches us to not rise up defensively concerning our own feelings, but to let God fight our battles in accordance to his purpose. Meekness teaches us to not seek recognition, but to allow God to exalt us.

2 Chronicles 20:15

15 And he said, Hearken ye, all Judah, and ye inhabitants of Jerusalem, and thou king Jehoshaphat, Thus saith the LORD unto you, Be not afraid nor dismayed by reason of this great multitude; for the battle is not yours, but God's. 215

Psalm 37:11

11 But the meek shall inherit the earth; and shall delight themselves in the abundance of peace. 216

215*The King James Version*, (Cambridge: Cambridge) 1769.
216*The King James Version*, (Cambridge: Cambridge) 1769.

143

The last element of the third cluster of the fruit of the Spirit is temperance. Temperance is self-control, which is being able to control one's thoughts and actions.

The lack of self-control has brought about the fall of kings and tycoons. These men can command armies, but cannot control themselves. It has been said that triumph and defeat is not in the crowded streets, nor in the shouts or applause of the crowd, but within ourselves.

The lack of self-control stems from one's physical appetite and mental habit (food, drugs, sex, and anger). Paul described this lack of control as being dominated by the sinful nature of the flesh.

Romans 8:5

5 Those who are dominated by the sinful nature think about sinful things, but those who are controlled by the Holy Spirit think about things that please the Spirit. 217

Proverbs 16:32

32 It is better to be patient than powerful; it is better to have self-control than to conquer a city. 218

Proverbs 25:28

28 A person without self-control is as defenseless as a city with broken-down walls. 219

217*Holy Bible, New Living Translation*, (Wheaton, IL: Tyndale House Publishers, Inc.) 1996.
218*Holy Bible, New Living Translation*, (Wheaton, IL: Tyndale House Publishers, Inc.) 1996.
219*Holy Bible, New Living Translation*, (Wheaton, IL: Tyndale House Publishers, Inc.) 1996.

We are in a time where sex, gambling, money, food, alcohol, and drugs are the cause of many of our social ills. We are in a society where violence, selfishness, apathy, and undisciplined living threaten to destroy us. It is imperative that we as Christians set an example for the world. We have to be the anchor in a raging sea. Many of us have sung the song "On Christ the Solid Rock I Stand"; well now it is time to demonstrate this rock to the world through temperance and self-control.

Part 3 • Gifts of the Spirit

Purpose of the Gifts

I have intentionally left the study of the gifts of the Spirit last in the book. The reason is because I wanted to put the emphasis on the fruit of the Spirit. If we recognize that our ultimate purpose on this earth is to win souls, then we must recognize that that purpose will best be accomplished when the fruit of the Spirit is being demonstrated in our lives.

Paul makes the case for me in his letter to the Corinthians who were caught up in spiritual gifts:

1 Corinthians 13:1-3

Though I speak with the tongues of men and of angels, and have not charity, I am become as sounding brass, or a tinkling cymbal. 2 And though I have the gift of prophecy, and understand all mysteries, and all knowledge; and though I have all faith, so that I could remove mountains, and have not charity, I am nothing. 3 And though I bestow all my goods to feed the poor, and though I give my body to be burned, and have not charity, it profiteth me nothing. 220

Simply put, Paul says here, if he had the spiritual gifts of speaking in tongues, prophecy, knowledge, faith, and mercy, but did not have charity (love), then he would be useless. He would be useless in accomplishing his true purpose.

I'm not aware of very many Christians who have won their unsaved coworkers to Christ by speaking in tongues to them. They probably scared them away. But I have known

---

220*The King James Version*, (Cambridge: Cambridge) 1769.

many Christians who have won coworkers to Christ by showing and demonstrating love.

That being said, God did give us these gifts, so there must be a purpose for them. The gifts of the Holy Spirit are listed in the Holy Bible in Romans 12:6-8, 1 Corinthians 12:8-10, Ephesians 4:11, and 1 Peter 4:10-11. We will now study them, so that we can have a proper understanding of their purpose.

When we look at the word purpose, it means intent, design, mission, reason, or objective. So what did God intend when he gave us gifts of the Spirit? What was the mission or objective? What was the reason?

1 Corinthians 12:7

7 But the manifestation of the Spirit is given to every man to profit withal. 221

I like this passage much better in the "New Living Translation". It really shows us the purpose of the gifts of the Spirit.

1 Corinthians 12:7

7 A spiritual gift is given to each of us as a means of helping the entire church. 222

I will go into more detail later concerning the purpose of each gift, but I want to take some time and explain to you why understanding purpose in general is so important.

221*The King James Version*, (Cambridge: Cambridge) 1769.
222*Holy Bible, New Living Translation*, (Wheaton, IL: Tyndale House Publishers, Inc.) 1996.

If a person is given something, but does not understand its true purpose, they could end up hurting themselves or someone else with it. If we don't understand the true purpose of the gifts that God has given us, then we will end up misusing or abusing them.

We made this point earlier, but let's look at an example of how abuse can happen when we don't understand true purpose. If a man thought that the purpose of a wife was to be his house slave, to answer his every need; he would end up misusing and abusing her. When we don't understand the true purpose of the gifts of the Holy Spirit, we can end up misusing them, and hurting others in the process.

Responsibility to the Body of Christ

The first thing we really need to understand concerning the purpose of the gifts of the Holy Spirit is responsibility. Let us go back and look at the 12th chapter of 1st Corinthians.

1 Corinthians 12:7-11

7 A spiritual gift is given to each of us as a means of helping the entire church. 8 To one person the Spirit gives the ability to give wise advice; to another he gives the gift of special knowledge. 9 The Spirit gives special faith to another, and to someone else he gives the power to heal the sick. 10 He gives one person the power to perform miracles, and to another the ability to prophesy. He gives someone else the ability to know whether it is really the Spirit of God or another spirit that is speaking. Still another person is given the ability to speak in unknown languages, and another is given the ability to interpret what is being said. 11 It is the one and only

Holy Spirit who distributes these gifts. He alone decides which gift each person should have. 223

According to this passage of scripture, every Christian is given at least one spiritual gift. It is given to him or her to help the entire church, and it is given at the discretion of the Holy Spirit. We are responsible for the gifts that we are given. We have a responsibility to exercise our gifts to benefit or help the church.

Just as my two legs are responsible for getting my body from place to place, those who are the legs in the body of Christ, have the responsibility of getting the church from place to place. Paul makes this very point in the following passages.

1 Corinthians 12:12-27

12 The human body has many parts, but the many parts make up only one body. So it is with the body of Christ. 13 Some of us are Jews, some are Gentiles, some are slaves, and some are free. But we have all been baptized into Christ's body by one Spirit, and we have all received the same Spirit. 14 Yes, the body has many different parts, not just one part. 15 If the foot says, "I am not a part of the body because I am not a hand," that does not make it any less a part of the body. 16 And if the ear says, "I am not part of the body because I am only an ear and not an eye," would that make it any less a part of the body? 17 Suppose the whole body were an eye— then how would you hear? Or if your whole body were just one big ear, how could you smell anything? 18 But God made our bodies with many parts, and he has put each part just where he wants it. 19 What a strange thing a body would be if it had only one part! 20 Yes, there are many parts, but only

---

223*Holy Bible, New Living Translation*, (Wheaton, IL: Tyndale House Publishers, Inc.) 1996.

one body. 21 The eye can never say to the hand, "I don't need you." The head can't say to the feet, "I don't need you." 22 In fact, some of the parts that seem weakest and least important are really the most necessary. 23 And the parts we regard as less honorable are those we clothe with the greatest care. So we carefully protect from the eyes of others those parts that should not be seen, 24 while other parts do not require this special care. So God has put the body together in such a way that extra honor and care are given to those parts that have less dignity. 25 This makes for harmony among the members, so that all the members care for each other equally. 26 If one part suffers, all the parts suffer with it, and if one part is honored, all the parts are glad. 27 Now all of you together are Christ's body, and each one of you is a separate and necessary part of it. 224

Purpose is not Proof!

Many people have used the manifestation of the gifts of the Spirit as proof that they have the Holy Spirit. Let's get one thing straight. The Holy Bible has never said that we were to use the gifts of the Spirit to prove that we have the Holy Spirit. My legs, which are part of my body, do not have to prove to me that they are legs; they simply have to just do their job to benefit my body.

Ephesians 4:11-16

11 And he gave some, apostles; and some, prophets; and some, evangelists; and some, pastors and teachers; 12 For the perfecting of the saints, for the work of the ministry, for the edifying of the body of Christ: 13 Till we all come in

---

224*Holy Bible, New Living Translation*, (Wheaton, IL: Tyndale House Publishers, Inc.) 1996.

the unity of the faith, and of the knowledge of the Son of God, unto a perfect man, unto the measure of the stature of the fulness of Christ: 14 That we henceforth be no more children, tossed to and fro, and carried about with every wind of doctrine, by the sleight of men, and cunning craftiness, whereby they lie in wait to deceive; 15 But speaking the truth in love, may grow up into him in all things, which is the head, even Christ: 16 From whom the whole body fitly joined together and compacted by that which every joint supplieth, according to the effectual working in the measure of every part, maketh increase of the body unto the edifying of itself in love. 225

Verse 12 again gives us the true purpose of the gifts, to perfect (help, benefit) the saints, the ministry, and the body of Christ (the church). There is nothing here that talks about proof. As a matter of fact, the only time we see the Holy Bible making reference to proof is when it is referring to fruit.

John 15:2

2 Every branch in me that beareth not fruit he taketh away: and every branch that beareth fruit, he purgeth it, that it may bring forth more fruit. 226

Purpose is not Jealousy!

We are not to covet or be jealous of the gifts that others have. Why? Because the gifts that we have, have nothing to do with us, and everything to do with God's purpose! Let us look again at Paul's letter to the Corinthians.

225*The King James Version,* (Cambridge: Cambridge) 1769.
226*The King James Version,* (Cambridge: Cambridge) 1769.

1 Corinthians 12:11

11 But all these worketh that one and the selfsame Spirit, dividing to every man severally as he will. 227

1 Corinthians 12:11

11 All these are activated by one and the same Spirit, who allots to each one individually just as the Spirit chooses. 228

We don't chose our gifts, the Holy Spirit does. He does it according to the will of God. So we should not be jealous of gifts that we see in others and not in ourselves. We should just thank God for the gift he's given us, and exercise it to its fullest. Whatever gift or gifts we have were given to us according to God's purpose

Romans 8:28

28 And we know that all things work together for good to them that love God, to them who are the called according to his purpose. 229

I personally have the gifts of pastoring and teaching. I thank God for them and I use them to their fullest. God has also sent others to our church with other gifts. The intent is that I use mine, and they use theirs, and all in the body of Christ benefit. As Christians, we get in trouble when a person who is an "ARM" is trying to be a "LEG". We also get in trouble when the person who is a "FOOT" is insisting that everyone else be a "FOOT"! Both of these points are wrong

---

227*The King James Version*, (Cambridge: Cambridge) 1769.
228*The New Revised Standard Version*, (Nashville, TN:
Thomas Nelson Publishers) 1989.
229*The King James Version*, (Cambridge: Cambridge) 1769.

and are not supported in the Holy Bible! We all have to accept whatever gifts God has given us and begin to use them.

Discovering and Recognizing Your Gifts

I have two mottos that I think will help every Christian with purpose as it relates to the Holy Spirit. They show the contrasting differences between the gifts of the Spirit and the fruit of the Spirit.

The first motto is "gifts of the Spirit are for the church, and fruit of the Spirit is for the unsaved". The gifts are used to strengthen the church. The fruit is used to draw the unsaved.

The second motto is "gifts of the Spirit are used to make us more like Christ and fruit of the Spirit is the evidence that we are becoming more like him". If we are not producing fruit, then we are not properly using our gifts.

There are over 20 spiritual gifts mentioned in the Holy Bible in Romans 12:6-8, 1 Corinthians 12:8-10, Ephesians 4:11, and 1 Peter 4:10-11. These gifts can be categorized into three groups; they are the foundation gifts (apostles, prophets, evangelist, pastors, teachers), the works gifts (wisdom, knowledge, faith, discerning of spirits, helps, and administrations), and the sign gifts (healings, miracles, and tongues).

"Stir Up" Your Gifts

How are we to discover or recognize our gifts? This is a very important point, because before we can use our gifts, we must first know what they are! We must stir up whatever gifts are in us!

2 Timothy 1:6-7

6 Wherefore I put thee in remembrance that thou stir up the gift of God, which is in thee by the putting on of my hands. 7 For God hath not given us the spirit of fear; but of power, and of love, and of a sound mind. 230

This passage uses the words "stir up!" When you add sugar to unsweetened iced tea, the sugar goes straight to the bottom. The sugar will be in the tea, but if it's not stirred up, when you drink the tea, it will taste bitter. Our spiritual gifts have to be stirred up, activated, put to use, or we will be bitter. Just as the unstirred sugar will not make the tea taste better, the unstirred spiritual gifts will leave us ineffective as Christians.

In other words, we need to get to work. We need to start moving, start doing, start helping, start asking, start volunteering, and start working! The more we do, the more the gifts will be stirred up in us. As a pastor, I've often seen people sit around in church doing nothing. One excuse I hear a lot is that they are just waiting on God. In reality, they probably didn't know what their gift was and so simply did nothing. Another excuse I hear is that there is nothing for them to do. Well Satan is making sinners everyday, and as long as there are sinners in this world, there is something for us to do!

When I first became a minister, I remember going to my pastor and telling him that I didn't know what my calling was as a minister. Other ministers at the church would say that they were called to be a pastor, an evangelist, or some other lofty ministerial role; but I didn't have a clue for myself. My pastor told me these words and I've never forgotten them. He said to simply operate in the gift of helps. He was telling me to just get busy and do whatever I see needs to be done.

230*The King James Version*, (Cambridge: Cambridge) 1769.

When we simply get to work, we will stir up the gifts that are in us, and they will come forth. As we are working in the church, trying this ministry or that ministry, we will see the things that we are good in and our gifts will emerge. However, if we sit around waiting, we may never discover our spiritual gifts and God will not be pleased with us because we are commanded to use our gifts!

1 Timothy 4:14-16

14 Do not neglect the spiritual gift you received through the prophecies spoken to you when the elders of the church laid their hands on you. 15 Give your complete attention to these matters. Throw yourself into your tasks so that everyone will see your progress. 16 Keep a close watch on yourself and on your teaching. Stay true to what is right, and God will save you and those who hear you. 231

Pray for Direction

Proverbs 3:5-6

5 Trust in the LORD with all thine heart; and lean not unto thine own understanding. 6 In all thy ways acknowledge him, and he shall direct thy paths. 232

Once we begin to work, we must pray to God for direction. This direction will lead us to where we need to be and what we need to be doing to exercise our gifts. If Michael Jordan only played baseball and never tried-out for the basketball team, we may have never experienced one of the

---

231*Holy Bible, New Living Translation*, (Wheaton, IL: Tyndale House Publishers, Inc.) 1996.
232*The King James Version*, (Cambridge: Cambridge) 1769.

greatest basketball players that ever lived. One year he was even cut from the basketball team, but he kept on trying. The reason why we must work in the church and do whatever we see that needs to be done is because we may be the next Michael Jordan of the Spiritual world.

Pay Attention to People

I make this point somewhat advisedly, because people can both help you and hurt you in this area. Sometimes people will tell you that you have this gift or that gift, and before you know it, you are out on a limb that's about to be sawed off! I believe that many ministers have gone into pastoring not because they had the gift, but because someone told them they were a good preacher. They may or may not have been a good preacher, but that has nothing to do with whether or not they had the gift of pastoring. Many of them got out on the wrong limb, and never recovered.

On the other hand, people can help you in discovering your spiritual gifts. For example, you may not be aware of an ability to be a good listener and counselor, but time after time you notice that people are always coming to you with their problems. Whether they know it or not, these people have recognized something in you that helps them. It's a spiritual gift from God!

The process of discovering your specific spiritual gifts may be a lengthy one. Some gifts may not emerge for years. Some gifts may not emerge until we are confronted with opportunities. Other gifts may not emerge until we are confronted with challenges or problems. But we cannot become discouraged, because as long as we are still alive then we know that God has a purpose for us, and that he is going to use the gifts that he has placed in us.

Foundation Gifts

In the previous chapter we categorized the gifts of the Spirit into three Groups; the foundation gifts (apostles, prophets, evangelist, pastors, teachers), the works gifts (wisdom, knowledge, faith, discerning of spirits, helps, and administrations), and the sign gifts (healings, miracles, and tongues). Let us now look at the foundation gifts.

The foundation gifts are the group of gifts that establish the groundwork, infrastructure, and underpinning for the body of Christ.

Matthew 16:18

18 And I say also unto thee, That thou art Peter, and upon this rock I will build my church; and the gates of hell shall not prevail against it. 233

Jesus in this passage established the foundation for the Church, and declared that even the gates of hell could not prevail against it.

2 Timothy 2:19

19 Nevertheless the foundation of God standeth sure, having this seal, The Lord knoweth them that are his. And, Let every one that nameth the name of Christ depart from iniquity. 234

233*The King James Version*, (Cambridge: Cambridge) 1769.
234*The King James Version*, (Cambridge: Cambridge) 1769.

When a child is born, it is very important that the baby has a solid foundation. The foundation represents the things that are provided to the child to give it a good start in life. Love, support, food, protection, and nurturing are all things that are provided to that child to make sure he or she starts out life with a solid foundation. But even before birth, the foundation must be established. The mother must take care of herself. She must refrain from the use of alcohol, drugs, and smoking. She is encouraged to eat properly and exercise. If the foundation is not properly established at the beginning, the body has a built in natural process to abort the human embryo.

The Holy Spirit gives us the foundation gifts to setup a healthy foundation for the body of Christ. These gifts help and teach us how to get rid of the substances that will hurt the foundation, and gives us the things that will strengthen the foundation.

Again, the foundation gifts are the apostles, prophets, evangelist, pastors, and teachers. The individuals with these gifts are those that are sent with a commission, a charge, or a mission.

Apostles

Apostles are used in 3 forms in the New Testament of the Holy Bible. The first form of the apostle is the general or basic form that applies to all Christians.

John 17:18

18 As thou hast sent me into the world, even so have I also sent them into the world. 235

235*The King James Version*, (Cambridge: Cambridge) 1769.

Matthew 28:19

19 Go ye therefore, and teach all nations, baptizing them in the name of the Father, and of the Son, and of the Holy Ghost: 236

The second form of the apostle used in the New Testament is the apostles of the church that were used as messengers who were sent on particular errands from one church to another. Paul would often do this with people like Titus and Epaphroditus.

The third form of the apostle used in the New Testament was for those that were given the gift of apostleship by the Holy Spirit. This form refers to that small and special group of men who were 'apostles of Christ', consisting of the twelve (Luke 6.12,13), and Paul (Gal 1:1).

Luke 6:12-13

12 And it came to pass in those days, that he went out into a mountain to pray, and continued all night in prayer to God. 13 And when it was day, he called unto him his disciples: and of them he chose twelve, whom also he named apostles; 237

Galatians 1:1

Paul, an apostle, (not of men, neither by man, but by Jesus Christ, and God the Father, who raised him from the dead;) 238

236*The King James Version*, (Cambridge: Cambridge) 1769.
237*The King James Version*, (Cambridge: Cambridge) 1769.
238*The King James Version*, (Cambridge: Cambridge) 1769.

These men were unique. They were chosen by Christ, and were eyewitnesses of the risen Lord. In the strictest sense, they have no successors. Apostles of today fall under the first or secondary form of missionaries listed earlier.

Prophets

The purpose of the prophet is not to be a psychic or talk to the dead. Although those with the gift of prophecy may foretell, the actual definition of the prophet is a public expounder. It is one who has a supernatural ability to communicate God's Words to man. The prophet also gives edification, instruction, consolation, and exhortation to the believers of the body of Christ. Since prophets have a supernatural ability of communications with God for the benefit of man, then this ability will consist of foretelling and predictive prophecy. The purpose is to tell the church what is to come.

One of the main missions or purposes of the prophet was to write the cannon of Holy Scripture that we call the Holy Bible today. Now since the Holy Bible has been completed, there is no more revelation of new truth. As a matter of fact, prophecy given to us today must be backed up with the Holy Bible. We should now look to the gift of prophecy for instruction, exhortation, rebuke, and warning of judgment.

Evangelist

To evangelize means to announce the good news of Jesus Christ. This word is actually only used 3 times in the New Testament. Luke called Philip an evangelist in Acts

21:8, Paul described it as a gift in Eph 4:11, and Paul urged Timothy to do the work of an evangelist in 2 Timothy 4:5.

The gift of evangelism is simply a gift of communicating the gospel. The evangelist is a messenger with a message centered on the death, burial, and resurrection of Jesus Christ.

Many churches have diminished their effectiveness by not recognizing the gift of evangelism. The evangelist speaks to the intellect and may not produce emotion. Many times this gift is accompanied with the gift of teaching. We must be careful that we don't spend too much time trying to see/expect visible results.

1 Corinthians 3:7

7 So then neither is he that planteth any thing, neither he that watereth; but God that giveth the increase. 239

We've got to remember that the battle is not ours; it's the Lord's. The Holy Bible does not teach us to seek after results. An evangelist is never rebuked because of meager results. Noah preached righteousness for 120 years, but he was only able to save his immediate family.

This gift is not limited to professionals: those who do it for a living. It is also given to lay members. Philip is the only person in the Holy Bible who was called an evangelist, and he was a deacon.

Pastor

239The King James Version, (Cambridge: Cambridge) 1769.

The Holy Bible does not often use the word pastor. It is only mentioned once in the New Testament, and its Hebrew translation is Shepherd. It is very important that Pastors operate as a shepherd and not as a hireling.

John 10:11-13

11 I am the good shepherd: the good shepherd giveth his life for the sheep. 12 But he that is an hireling, and not the shepherd, whose own the sheep are not, seeth the wolf coming, and leaveth the sheep, and fleeth: and the wolf catcheth them, and scattereth the sheep. 13 The hireling fleeth, because he is an hireling, and careth not for the sheep. 240

John 10:11-13

11 "I am the good shepherd. The good shepherd lays down his life for the sheep. 12 A hired hand will run when he sees a wolf coming. He will leave the sheep because they aren't his and he isn't their shepherd. And so the wolf attacks them and scatters the flock. 13 The hired hand runs away because he is merely hired and has no real concern for the sheep. 241

The gift of being a pastor includes gifts of counseling, guiding, warning, and guarding. In many respects youth counselors, Sunday school teachers, youth leaders, Holy Bible teachers, and assistants to the Pastor actually perform functions that are part of the pastoral gift. Thousands of people have this gift, and never become pastors, but use it to assist their Pastor and church.

240*The King James Version*, (Cambridge: Cambridge) 1769.
241*Holy Bible, New Living Translation*, (Wheaton, IL: Tyndale House Publishers, Inc.) 1996.

Teacher

A teacher is an instructor. This gift is extremely important in establishing the foundation of the church because once a person accepts Christ and becomes saved; they must then be instructed on what to do.

Matthew 28:19

19 Go ye therefore, and teach all nations, baptizing them in the name of the Father, and of the Son, and of the Holy Ghost: 242

If there is anything that the church needs more of, it is good competent teachers of the Word of God.

Hosea 4:6

6 My people are destroyed for lack of knowledge: because thou hast rejected knowledge, I will also reject thee, that thou shalt be no priest to me: seeing thou hast forgotten the law of thy God, I will also forget thy children. 243

Somebody said all we need is a little more love. But I say what we need is a few more people that will teach the real meaning of love according to the Holy Bible. Since God is love, we need more of God, and thus more people who can teach us about him.

242*The King James Version*, (Cambridge: Cambridge) 1769.
243*The King James Version*, (Cambridge: Cambridge) 1769.

Works Gifts

The second group of gifts is the works gifts. This group includes the gifts of wisdom, knowledge, faith, discerning of spirits, helps, and administrations. They are listed in a couple of passages in the Holy Bible!

1 Corinthians 12:8

8 For to one is given by the Spirit the word of wisdom; to another the word of knowledge by the same Spirit; 244

1 Corinthians 12:28

28 And God hath set some in the church, first apostles, secondarily prophets, thirdly teachers, after that miracles, then gifts of healings, helps, governments, diversities of tongues. 245

Since those gifted in the foundation group of gifts are used to establish the foundation of the church, those gifted in the works group of gifts are used to help build the church upon that foundation. They are the worker-bees who carry out the work of the church.

The foundation is the beginning of a building project not the end. No one ever builds a foundation and then quits to admire it. Its only purpose is to support the building that will be built on top of it, and so is the relationship between the foundation gifts and the works gifts. The foundation gifts establish a foundation for the works gifts to build the church. A person who has a foundation gift, such as a prophet or

---

244*The King James Version*, (Cambridge: Cambridge) 1769.
245*The King James Version*, (Cambridge: Cambridge) 1769.

pastor, should never become arrogant and think it is about them. They are here to establish the foundation so that those with the works gifts can build the church.

On the other hand, those with gifts in the works group should not depend on the pastor to do all the work in the church. Many times our churches are ineffective because the workers, those gifted with the works gifts, are leaving their responsibility to the pastor. It does the body of Christ no good if the pastor establishes the foundation, and then the workers never build the building.

In some ways, those that have gifts in the works group are more important than some of the more "flashier" gifts of prophesy, miracles, and healings.

1 Corinthians 12:20-27

20 Yes, there are many parts, but only one body. 21 The eye can never say to the hand, "I don't need you." The head can't say to the feet, "I don't need you." 22 In fact, some of the parts that seem weakest and least important are really the most necessary. 23 And the parts we regard as less honorable are those we clothe with the greatest care. So we carefully protect from the eyes of others those parts that should not be seen, 24 while other parts do not require this special care. So God has put the body together in such a way that extra honor and care are given to those parts that have less dignity. 25 This makes for harmony among the members, so that all the members care for each other equally. 26 If one part suffers, all the parts suffer with it, and if one part is honored, all the parts are glad. 27 Now all of you together are Christ's body, and each one of you is a separate and necessary part of it. 246

246*Holy Bible, New Living Translation*, (Wheaton, IL: Tyndale House Publishers, Inc.) 1996.

Wisdom & Knowledge

These two gifts are listed together here because you shouldn't have one without the other. If I'm to be wise, I must have information, knowledge on the subject. If I have information (knowledge), but don't know how to apply it (Wisdom), it does me no good.

Have you ever seen a person that was highly educated, but has no "street sense"? They can tell you about all the theoretical concepts and theories on a subject, but can't apply them to real life. I've known "sinners" who can quote many scriptures in the Holy Bible, sometimes more than Christians, but never apply them to their own lives.

The definition of spiritual gifts is a supernatural ability to perform a task, an ability that surpasses human ability.

There are three types of wisdom; human or natural wisdom, wisdom that is derived from education and experience, and wisdom that comes from God.

All of us are born with a certain amount of wisdom. Some things are just natural or instinctual to us. Others become wiser through experience and education. But a third group of individuals receive wisdom that cannot be explained through human means. It comes directly from God, and it is supernatural.

God is the first and the last, beginning and ending, the source of everything. The Holy Spirit gives a special supernatural gift of wisdom to some as God sees fit.

Wisdom is the ability to make correct decisions on the basis of knowledge. I sometimes go through an exercise with the executive staff of our ministry where I ask the group their opinion. I do this for two reasons. First of all, any leader that thinks that he or she knows it all is a fool. A good leader will surround himself with good knowledgeable people who can offer advice. More importantly however, I go through this exercise because some in the group may possess the gift of wisdom.

In order to be wise, a person must have information, knowledge to act upon. The gift of knowledge is the supernatural possession of information. People with this gift get information or knowledge that cannot be explained by human means. They don't get this knowledge from reading it, or from anyone telling it to them; it comes directly from God.

It is important to the body of Christ that these two gifts are in operation at the church. Many times a person will find himself or herself confused or unsure about a decision that needs to be made. It is at that point that those with the gift of wisdom step in to provide assistance. Other times a person may be getting ready to make a decision, but do not have all the information. For example, an individual may be planning to take a new job but doesn't know that the company will fold in three months. A person with the gift of knowledge could be put in a position to give them a supernatural word of knowledge.

Faith

Every Christian must have some measure of faith. Faith is necessary in order to become a Christian.

Hebrews 11:1

1 What is faith? It is the confident assurance that what we hope for is going to happen. It is the evidence of things we cannot yet see. 247

Hebrews 11:6

6 So, you see, it is impossible to please God without faith. Anyone who wants to come to him must believe that there is a God and that he rewards those who sincerely seek him. 248

The only way to get saved is through faith. However, the Holy Bible does indicate that we have different measures or levels of faith.

Romans 12:3

3 For I say, through the grace given unto me, to every man that is among you, not to think of himself more highly than he ought to think; but to think soberly, according as God hath dealt to every man the measure of faith. 249

Matthew 8:25-26

25 And his disciples came to him, and awoke him, saying, Lord, save us: we perish. 26 And he saith unto them, Why are ye fearful, O ye of little faith? Then he arose, and rebuked the winds and the sea; and there was a great calm. 250

247*Holy Bible, New Living Translation*, (Wheaton, IL: Tyndale House Publishers, Inc.) 1996.
248*Holy Bible, New Living Translation*, (Wheaton, IL: Tyndale House Publishers, Inc.) 1996.
249*The King James Version*, (Cambridge: Cambridge) 1769.
250*The King James Version*, (Cambridge: Cambridge) 1769.

All of us have some level or measure of this faith referred to in the previous verses. This faith is believing in what God has promised us in his word. However there is another type of faith that is a supernatural gift from the Holy Spirit. This is a gift that God gives some of us to have faith in things in which there is no specific promise from the Word of God.

When my wife and I started Victorious Praise Fellowship church, we were led to promote a major concert in our city. We were not concert promoters; we didn't have much money, and only had about 10 members at the time. The cost of the concert was going to be $17,000. Now there is no word in the Holy Bible for dealing with concerts. So concerning this event, I had no scripture to stand on and have faith in. But I knew in my heart that we were led to promote this concert.

One week before the concert, we had sold less than a hundred tickets. At $15 a ticket, you do that math! My heart sunk when Ticket Master gave me the bad news of the meager ticket sales. However, rather than stay down, the church members and I begin to pray. God again gave me a sense that everything would work out fine.

The concert was scheduled for Sunday evening, but by the Friday before the event, the ticket count had only reached a little above 200 tickets sold. Since I knew that God had led us to put on this concert, I simply believed that the people would show up at the door to purchase tickets on the day of the event. Well we are in Durham, NC, and in this area of the south, people do not like doing anything in the rain. On the day of the concert, it was raining "cats and dogs". It was one of those heavy rainy days where the sky was covered with dark clouds. Thoughts began to flood my mind; "no one is going to come out in this rain".

Well that morning, we had our normal Sunday morning service and God really blessed us. I was personally praying however that by the end of service the rain would stop and the people would come to the concert. To my dismay, it was still raining at the end of service. By then it was about 2:30pm, and the concert was at 6:00pm that evening. I left the service and went to Kinkos to pick up a 1000+ programs. Although the pre-ticketed sales and the rain discouraged me, somehow I was still led to pick up the programs for a 1000+ people.

By 5:30pm that evening, I had picked up the programs, gotten dressed, and was on my way to the concert hall. The rain had just stopped, and I didn't know what to expect. "Surely anyone who was thinking about coming to the concert had already given up because of the rain", was the thought that was racing through my head. But when I pulled up to the concert hall, there was a line of people going around the block waiting to get in. By the time the concert started and I walked out to speak, the hall was full.

It was one of the greatest moments of my life. God had proven himself to me in spite of all odds. In my mind, everything that could have gone wrong did; and yet the concert was a success. The only thing I had to keep me going when everything else around me was falling apart was a supernatural assurance of faith that God had given me.

You can't make yourself have the gift of faith. It's a gift that God has either given to you or not. If it is not God's will to do a thing for you, then your faith level cannot change that fact.

When people make reference to increasing your measure of faith, do not confuse this with the gift of faith.

Remember, gifts are given and not earned. The only type of faith we can affect and increase in our lives is faith in God's Word.

Romans 10:17

17 So then faith cometh by hearing, and hearing by the Word of God. 251

If you meditate and hide God's Word in your heart, you will have much faith. If you don't study his word, then you will have little faith. But the gift of faith only comes from God through the Holy Spirit when God wants to assure us of something that is not written in his word. If God has not specifically given you a measure of supernatural faith to put on a $17,000 concert with only a 10-member church, then you probably might not want to do it. Just because he gave it to me doesn't mean that he has given it to you.

Discernment of Spirits

The Hebrew translation for discernment embodies the idea of examining, understanding, or judging closely. The gift of discerning of spirits is a supernatural ability to distinguish spirits.

2 Corinthians 11:14-15

14 And no marvel; for Satan himself is transformed into an angel of light. 15 Therefore it is no great thing if his ministers also be transformed as the ministers of righteousness; whose end shall be according to their works. 252

251*The King James Version*, (Cambridge: Cambridge) 1769.
252*The King James Version*, (Cambridge: Cambridge) 1769.

Those who possess foundation gifts (apostles, prophets, evangelist, pastors, teachers) are people who tell us what God has said to them for the rest of us. This presents an inherent problem for the body of Christ. How can we determine if the person claiming to be speaking on behalf of God truly is speaking his will?

1 John 4:1-3

1 Dear friends, do not believe everyone who claims to speak by the Spirit. You must test them to see if the spirit they have comes from God. For there are many false prophets in the world. 2 This is the way to find out if they have the Spirit of God: If a prophet acknowledges that Jesus Christ became a human being, that person has the Spirit of God. 3 If a prophet does not acknowledge Jesus, that person is not from God. Such a person has the spirit of the Antichrist. You have heard that he is going to come into the world, and he is already here. 253

Yes, there are wolves in sheep's clothing, false prophets, evangelists, and pastors who are merely hirelings. They walk, talk, preach, teach, and go to church right along with the rest of us.

Matthew 13:24-30

24 Here is another story Jesus told: "The Kingdom of Heaven is like a farmer who planted good seed in his field. 25 But that night as everyone slept, his enemy came and planted weeds among the wheat. 26 When the crop began to grow and produce grain, the weeds also grew. 27 The farmer's servants

253*Holy Bible, New Living Translation*, (Wheaton, IL: Tyndale House Publishers, Inc.) 1996.

came and told him, 'Sir, the field where you planted that good seed is full of weeds!' 28 " 'An enemy has done it!' the farmer exclaimed. " 'Shall we pull out the weeds?' they asked. 29 "He replied, 'No, you'll hurt the wheat if you do. 30 Let both grow together until the harvest. Then I will tell the harvesters to sort out the weeds and burn them and to put the wheat in the barn.' " 254

God will eventually take care of the weeds, the wolves, the false prophets, and the hirelings. But what do we do in the interim? The Holy Bible teaches us that we should test spirits and doctrines against the standards of the Word of God. However, God gives some individuals extraordinary abilities to discern the truth. Christians with this gift then help the entire body as a check and balance against those that would deceive us.

Helps

The gift of helps is the supernatural ability of providing support and assistance to others. An apostle, evangelist, or pastor can never complete everything that God has given them. The vision is always bigger then the man that it is given to. That is why God always provides helpers.

God uses people who are available and willing. Every church I know is composed of two churches; an outer church of those who fill up the pews on Sunday morning, and an inner church of those who do all the work the other 6 days of the week. Most of those in the outer church have good intentions. Many of them even join the various ministries. But the problem is that they always seem to be busy when it's time to

---

254*Holy Bible, New Living Translation*, (Wheaton, IL: Tyndale House Publishers, Inc.) 1996.

work. The real work always ends up falling on the inner church workers.

This gift is about helping with the activities of the church so that those with other gifts can be released to utilize them more freely. If it is my job to pastor and teach, I will be less effective in that assignment if I also have to do church administration, teach the choir, play the organ, clean the church, and do the building maintenance. I will not have very much time or energy left to do the work I've really been called to do.

When my wife and I started our church, we did everything. We painted walls, cleaned the building, setup the chairs, did the administration, and more. As a former musician, I also played the organ, and taught songs to the choir. Almost every pastor that starts a ministry has to work like this. However, if that ministry is to ever truly grow and become effective, something will have to give. Either the pastor will get some help so that he can dedicate himself to his true calling; or the church will suffer and the pastor will die prematurely.

Although every Christian should have an active role in working in the body of Christ to further the Gospel, some of us have been given the gift of helps. Those that have this gift must understand the importance of their role. If the helpers are not in place, then the preachers, evangelists, and teachers will not be effective.

Administration

This gift is about the leadership and organization necessary to "get the job done"! When I worked in corporate America, a lot of attention was placed on engineers and computer scientist. Because of my computer science degree from Michigan State University, I was hired by a major fortune 500 company, and paid a great deal of money. However corporate America eventually found out that although they were hiring a lot of talented people, the jobs they were hiring these people to do were not getting done on time or within budget. The problem was not in talent of the people doing the work, but in the managers and administrators. Companies began to place a lot of focus on training and educating engineers and computer scientist to become project managers. They had people who understood the technology, but they needed people who could manage and administer it.

A church can have a lot of gifted and talented people, but may not reach it potential if there are no good administrators in place. The vision of the church may be given to the pastor, but it may actually take a good administrator to implement it. The administrators are the ones who manage the vision and make sure that it's implemented.

The Holy Bible teaches us that we must have administrative leadership. Jesus spent more than half his time in ministry with his disciples. Why? He had to teach them how to be leaders. Paul and Barnabas appointed elders in every church they formed to handle the day-to-day activities and keep the churches operating.

Hebrews 13:17

17 Obey them that have the rule over you, and submit yourselves: for they watch for your souls, as they that must give account, that they may do it with joy, and not with grief: for that is unprofitable for you. 255

255*The King James Version*, (Cambridge: Cambridge) 1769.

The administrative leaders must not be dictatorial, egotistical, or dogmatic. But they should be humble, gracious, courteous, kind, and filled with love.

All the gifts that fall into the works group are intended to help build the church on the foundation being setup by those that have gifts in the foundation group. The ultimate goal is to help promote the Kingdom of Heaven. God has given us these gifts and he expects us to develop and use them for his glory.

Sign Gifts

The sign gifts consist of healings, miracles, and speaking in tongues. By sign gifts, we mean those gifts of the Holy Spirit that are the obvious outward signs of the working of God.

These gifts seem to rate the most attention from us. They are exciting to the imagination, producing outward manifestations that attract multitudes. Many Christians will stay at home during mid week service because they claim they are too busy, but will go to a revival every night for a week if there is an evangelist that is performing healings or miracles.

Why this response? It is because we seem to be fascinated by the spectacular and the unusual. This type of curiosity is not necessarily good or helpful, but it is very common.

Isn't it an interesting point to note that in the four passages of scriptures where the gifts of the Spirit are discussed (Romans 12:6-8, 1 Corinthians 12:8-10, Ephesians 4:11, and 1 Peter 4:10-11), focus is placed on the sign gifts only in Paul's letter to the Corinthians. Note also that his writings here were a letter of rebuke that dealt with a church that was out of order, rebellious, sinful, and was abusing or misusing the gifts of the Spirit (especially speaking in tongues).

God did not give us these gifts to be misused, become divisive, or disrupt our fellowship. When these things occur, the greatest manifestation of the Spirit, love, is diminished.

1 Corinthians 13:1

Though I speak with the tongues of men and of angels, and have not charity, I am become as sounding brass, or a tinkling cymbal. 256

1 Corinthians 13:1

If I could speak in any language in heaven or on earth but didn't love others, I would only be making meaningless noise like a loud gong or a clanging cymbal. 257

The greatest thing God gave us was not speaking in tongues, it was not supernatural healings, and it was not the performing of miracles; but it was love.

However, the Holy Spirit did give us these gifts; it's just important that we not get caught up in them. This will be accomplished when we understand their true purpose.

Healings

The Holy Spirit gives the gift of healing (gift of cures) to some of us in the body of Christ for the benefit of the rest. There are many cases of healing in both the Old and New Testament. The New Testament is filled with instances where Jesus and his disciples healed the sick. In modern times, countless instances of physical healing, unexplained by modern medicine, have been recorded.

There are two types of healings expressed in the Christian world today; healing associated with the gift of healing, and healing where the emphasis is placed on one's faith. Some people say, "If you have enough faith, then you

---

256*The King James Version*, (Cambridge: Cambridge) 1769.
257*Holy Bible, New Living Translation*, (Wheaton, IL: Tyndale House Publishers, Inc.) 1996.

can be healed". But this type of healing takes the emphasis off the gift of healing and places it upon the sick individuals faith level.

There are people who refuse to go to a doctor because they believe that God will heal them without the doctor. Now unless they are operating in the gift of faith (see the earlier chapter on "Faith"), they may be misguided in the proper use of biblical faith. Jesus acknowledged the use and need of doctors himself in the following passage.

Mark 2:17

17 When Jesus heard this, he told them, "Healthy people don't need a doctor—sick people do. I have come to call sinners, not those who think they are already good enough." 258

That being said, we do see people in the Holy Bible being healed as a result of their faith.

Matthew 9:21-22

21 For she said within herself, If I may but touch his garment, I shall be whole. 22 But Jesus turned him about, and when he saw her, he said, Daughter, be of good comfort; thy faith hath made thee whole. And the woman was made whole from that hour. 259

But we also see people being healed in which there was no mention of faith.

Matthew 8:14-15

258*Holy Bible, New Living Translation*, (Wheaton, IL: Tyndale House Publishers, Inc.) 1996.
259*The King James Version*, (Cambridge: Cambridge) 1769.

14 When Jesus arrived at Peter's house, Peter's mother-in-law was in bed with a high fever. 15 But when Jesus touched her hand, the fever left her. Then she got up and prepared a meal for him. 260

So then God can heal through faith, he can heal through doctors, and he can heal through the gift of healing whether there is faith or not! So as Christians we should not put God in a box and limit him to only one form of healing. Remember, all gifts come from God! He may use the miracle of modern medicine and doctors to heal us. He may give us the supernatural gift of faith to assure us that he's going to heal us when the doctors have failed. Lastly, he may use a person who has the supernatural gift of healing to heal us.

We must also be open to the fact that it may not be the will of God that we be healed of all our illnesses. If God has not revealed to us that we are going to be healed; and if the doctors have not been able to help our illness, then we should simply pray that God's will be done.

The bottom line is that many Christians do suffer physical, mental, and even spiritual illnesses from time to time. Although God provides help to us for these illnesses, we must never lose sight on the true purpose of God's gifts. They are not necessarily for our selfish benefit, but for his purpose.

Romans 8:26-28

26 Likewise the Spirit also helpeth our infirmities: for we know not what we should pray for as we ought: but the Spirit itself maketh intercession for us with groanings which cannot be uttered. 27 And he that searcheth the hearts

---

260*Holy Bible, New Living Translation*, (Wheaton, IL: Tyndale House Publishers, Inc.) 1996.

knoweth what is the mind of the Spirit, because he maketh intercession for the saints according to the will of God. 28 And we know that all things work together for good to them that love God, to them who are the called according to his purpose. 261

Miracles

A miracle is an event produced beyond the power of any known physical law. A physical occurrence produced by the power of God, a wonder.

Why was this gift originally given to us? The apostles were asked the question "How do we know that you are what you say you are, and that your words are true?" What is the proof of your apostleship?

2 Corinthians 12:12

12 When I was with you, I certainly gave you every proof that I am truly an apostle, sent to you by God himself. For I patiently did many signs and wonders and miracles among you. 262

At strategic moments, God manifested himself to men by miracles so that they would have outward, confirming evidence that God was real.

There are certain sign gifts that were given to the apostles of the early church to authenticate their message. They had the gift of healing, could raise the dead, and speak in

---

261*The King James Version*, (Cambridge: Cambridge) 1769.
262*Holy Bible, New Living Translation*, (Wheaton, IL: Tyndale House Publishers, Inc.) 1996.

tongues. Paul had gone through the Galatian country, and there must have been fifty dialects and languages. Paul could speak them all. It was necessary to get the Word of God out into the Roman Empire in a hurry, and so these apostles were equipped with these gifts. So sign gifts were used as proof of a man's apostleship.

Should we look for Miracles as proof today?

John 14:12

12 Verily, verily, I say unto you, He that believeth on me, the works that I do shall he do also; and greater works than these shall he do; because I go unto my Father. 263

First of all, there were great men in the Holy Bible that performed no miracles:

Matthew 11:10-11

10 For this is he, of whom it is written, Behold, I send my messenger before thy face, which shall prepare thy way before thee. 11 Verily I say unto you, Among them that are born of women there hath not risen a greater than John the Baptist: notwithstanding he that is least in the kingdom of heaven is greater than he. 264

The honor that Jesus bestows on John the Baptist here is great. He says that there is no one born of women greater than John. However, isn't it very interesting that this great man, who was called to pave the way for Jesus Christ, performed no miracles?

263*The King James Version*, (Cambridge: Cambridge) 1769.
264*The King James Version*, (Cambridge: Cambridge) 1769.

184

John 10:41-42

41 And many resorted unto him, and said, John did no miracle: but all things that John spake of this man were true. 42 And many believed on him there. 265

Although miracles, signs, and wonders were used to help establish the early church, this was not the only method used by God to draw men to him. Our world today is very different than the world that existed during the formation of the early church. At the time of Jesus' death, most of the world had not heard of him. Today, Jesus is preached around the world, 24 hours a day on radio and television. Yes miracles are still performed today, but we don't use them as the early church did to spread the Gospel. They needed miracles; we have the written Word of God. They needed signs and wonders; we have faith in God's Word.

I've heard people say that there is a problem with the modern church because we don't see miracles as there were in biblical times. The implication is that since we don't see some of the spectacular miracles today as in times past, then the church must not be as committed or dedicated to God. But I don't believe this to be the case.

The churches of today are no more or less committed to God than they were in the past. Yes we have problems and issues in our churches today, but there were problems in churches of the past as well.

1 Corinthians 5:1-2

1 I can hardly believe the report about the sexual immorality going on among you, something so evil that even the pagans don't do it. I am told that you have a man in your

---

265*The King James Version*, (Cambridge: Cambridge) 1769.

church who is living in sin with his father's wife. 2 And you are so proud of yourselves! Why aren't you mourning in sorrow and shame? And why haven't you removed this man from your fellowship? 266

This immoral behavior existed in a church that was filled with people speaking in tongues, and apparently performing miracles. How could this be?

Romans 11:29

29 For the gifts and calling of God are without repentance. 267

Romans 11:29

29 For God's gifts and his call can never be withdrawn. 268

The reason these gifts were still in operation in spite of the behavior of the people is because a gift is given free of charge, and once God gives them, he does not take them away. However, the more important point here concerning gifts is God's purpose. Gifts were not given to us because of who we were but to accomplish God's purpose.

Some gifts are not as prevalent today as they were in times past because their purpose has been completed. If I give a person $1000 to paint my house this month, I don't need to give them another $1000 next month to paint my house.

266*Holy Bible, New Living Translation*, (Wheaton, IL: Tyndale House Publishers, Inc.) 1996.
267*The King James Version*, (Cambridge: Cambridge) 1769.
268*Holy Bible, New Living Translation*, (Wheaton, IL: Tyndale House Publishers, Inc.) 1996.

Why? Because my house is painted, that task has been completed.

The purpose of the gift of apostleship was to establish the church of Christ. When Jesus ascended back to heaven after his death and resurrection, there was no church, so we needed apostles to establish the church of Christ. We don't see the gift of apostleship operating that much in the United States today, because that purpose has been completed. In some cities, there are churches on every corner. We have the gospel being preached 24 hours a day on television and radio. We have van ministries, book ministries, tape ministries, and even Internet ministries. Clearly the purpose of establishing the church of Christ in this area has been completed. I'm not saying that our work is done; it's just that the house is already painted. Now it's time to cut the grass!

So the real reason that we may not see as many miracles today is because for the most point, their purpose has been completed. I'm not saying that God doesn't perform miracles today; I'm just saying that the purpose of the miracles in biblical times was to establish the church!

2 Corinthians 12:12

12 When I was with you, I certainly gave you every proof that I am truly an apostle, sent to you by God himself. For I patiently did many signs and wonders and miracles among you. 269

There was no church during these times, so Paul had to have these sign gifts to authenticate his apostleship in order to

---

269*Holy Bible, New Living Translation*, (Wheaton, IL: Tyndale House Publishers, Inc.) 1996.

establish the church. But today we do not walk by sight (sign gifts), but we walk by faith.

2 Corinthians 5:7

7 (For we walk by faith, not by sight:) 270

For us to depend on sign gifts as a basis of our relationship with God is an indication of spiritual immaturity. Although our churches today have many issues and problems, in some respects we have to have a degree of maturity that did not exist in the early churches. The first disciples actually walked with Jesus, they saw him. We have never seen Jesus; we have to accept him by faith. The early churches saw many miracles, but many modern Christians have seen few if any miracles. Again, we have to walk by faith and not by sight!

The Greatest Miracle

Miracles were used to advance the Gospel, but it's now advanced. So I believe that our expectation concerning miracles need to change.

John 14:12

12 Verily, verily, I say unto you, He that believeth on me, the works that I do shall he do also; and greater works than these shall he do; because I go unto my Father. 271

Jesus performed many works and miracles. He says here that we would do greater works. So what are these greater works? Some people believe that greater works mean that we would perform the same miracles Christ performed,

---

270*The King James Version*, (Cambridge: Cambridge) 1769.
271*The King James Version*, (Cambridge: Cambridge) 1769.

just more of them. In other words, we would heal more sick people, restore sight to more blind people, raise more people from the dead, and cast out more demons from the possessed. But this is not greater works; this is just more of the same.

I work out in the gym and lift weights. The most I've ever bench-pressed is 305 pounds. I've only done it once, but I've done it. Now if you bench-press 305 pounds 20 times, you have not lifted any more weight than I. If we were in a weight lifting competition, we would simply tie. The only way you would win (be greater) would be if you lifted 306 pounds, because then you would have lifted something that was greater.

So what would qualify as greater works in terms of the works that Jesus had done. It would be something that Jesus himself had never done!

Acts 2:14-16

14 But Peter, standing with the eleven, raised his voice and addressed them, "Men of Judea and all who live in Jerusalem, let this be known to you, and listen to what I say. 15 Indeed, these are not drunk, as you suppose, for it is only nine o'clock in the morning. 16 No, this is what was spoken through the prophet Joel: 272

Acts 2:37-41

37 Now when they heard this, they were cut to the heart and said to Peter and to the other apostles, "Brothers, what should we do?" 38 Peter said to them, "Repent, and be baptized every one of you in the name of Jesus Christ so that your sins may be forgiven; and you will receive the gift of the

---

272*The New Revised Standard Version,* (Nashville, TN: Thomas Nelson Publishers) 1989.

Holy Spirit.39 For the promise is for you, for your children, and for all who are far away, everyone whom the Lord our God calls to him."40 And he testified with many other arguments and exhorted them, saying, "Save yourselves from this corrupt generation."41 So those who welcomed his message were baptized, and that day about three thousand persons were added. 273

When Jesus was on the earth he would heal the sick, give sight to the blind, cause the lame to walk, cleanse the leper, and raise the dead. He would then say to them, "go and sin no more"!

But here, Peter didn't heal anyone, he didn't raise anyone from the dead, and he didn't cause the lame to walk. He simply preached the gospel of Jesus Christ, and 3000 souls were saved in one day. This is something that Jesus never did.

It is said, "Jesus did not come to preach the gospel, but he came that there might be a gospel to preach." When I accepted Christ, it was not because of a healing or a miracle, but it was because of the gospel. Many more people have been saved today as a result of the gospel than any other works. People have been saved even as a result of just watching the gospel being preached on television or hearing it on the radio. The transformation that occurs in men has to be the greatest miracle of all. And every time we share the gospel, we have the opportunity to cause the miracle of regeneration.

273*The New Revised Standard Version*, (Nashville, TN: Thomas Nelson Publishers) 1989.

Speaking in Tongues

I want to introduce the gift of speaking in tongues by sharing some stories that I read in a book written by Billy Graham concerning the Holy Spirit.

"A leading minister in the church of Scotland lay in ICU waiting to die. He begins to talk to the Lord, and as he did, he found himself praying in a language he had never heard. After confiding this to a friend, he never mentioned it again. He recovered to serve the Lord several more years."

"A frantic young wife and mother, for whom everything had gone wrong one day, sat up in bed that night literally fussing at God. Without ever hearing of it or asking for it, she begins to pray in tongues. She said that it felt as if she was out of her body, and when she came to, she looked at the clock thinking she had been praying for 30 minutes, but to her amazement it was dawn, and she was refreshed. Her burden had been lifted; the frustration, anger, and complaining were all gone, and she felt like she had had a good night's sleep."

"A Sunday school class was studying the Holy Spirit and begin to share: One class member testified about his experience and how he initially became totally preoccupied with tongues. Eventually he leveled off realizing that the Holy Spirit has been given to glorify Jesus in differing ways. Today he's a uniquely gifted minister. A second class member, who also claimed to speak in tongues, was expelled from college a few weeks later for open, repeated, and unrepentant immorality. A third class member told of being at a meeting where someone was speaking in tongues. He recognized the language spoken as a language he used to hear when he assisted his grandmother who was a spiritual medium."[274]

Each of the experiences in the last story about the Sunday school students illustrates three sources for what are called tongues. The first one was of the Holy Spirit, the second one was psychological influence, and the third was of satanic influences.

Now I don't claim to be an expert on the Holy Spirit and his gifts, and neither should any of us. However, one thing is for certain, the Holy Spirit and his gifts were not given to us to create division. There may be people, or even churches where tongues are prominent, but then again there may be just as many other people or churches where tongues are not.

What does the Holy Bible say?

For nearly a century, speaking in tongues has been given an important role among many Christians and certain churches. Some (old time Pentecostals) believe that following conversion, there should be tongue speaking. Some have went as far as to have classes to teach one how to speak in tongues. We also have thousands of "Charismatics" who are accepted as believers but have never spoken in tongues. To them, speaking in tongues is not regarded as an essential sign of having been born again. They believe that the Spirit took up his residence in their hearts at the time of regeneration.

So what does the Holy Bible have to say about speaking in tongues? First of all, it is mentioned in only two

---

[274] Stories taken from book, The Holy Spirit, by Billy Graham

New Testament books, the book of Acts and the first book of Corinthians.

In the book of Acts, speaking in tongues is mentioned three times in chapters 2, 10, and 19. All of the discussion of speaking in tongues in the book of Acts deal with the introduction of the Holy Spirit to three different groups: the Jews, the Gentiles, and the "John the Baptist" converts.

In the first book of Corinthians, the discussion on speaking in tongues is in chapters 12 and 14. The discussions in these chapters are in the form of instructions directly to the church.

We have already discussed speaking in tongues extensively as it relates to the book of Acts. Please review the chapters "The Introduction of the Holy Spirit", "Have you received the Holy Ghost since you believed?", and "Should every Christian Speak in Tongues?". The bottom line is that all the discussions of speaking in tongues in the book of Acts are not instructions to the church, but is a historical account about the introduction of the Holy Spirit to man. The first book of Corinthians, on the other hand, does give us specific instructions concerning speaking in tongues. So in trying to understand the role and purpose of speaking in tongues for the church, this is where we should look. We will spend the rest of this chapter studying Corinthians to learn exactly how we should treat the gift of speaking in tongues.

Instruction of Tongues in 1st Corinthians

The first book of Corinthians mentions two gifts concerning tongues, speaking in unknown tongues and interpretation of tongues.

1 Corinthians 12:10-11

10 He gives one person the power to perform miracles, and to another the ability to prophesy. He gives someone else the ability to know whether it is really the Spirit of God or another spirit that is speaking. Still another person is given the ability to speak in unknown languages, and another is given the ability to interpret what is being said. 11 It is the one and only Holy Spirit who distributes these gifts. He alone decides which gift each person should have. 275

The 11th verse here says that the Holy Spirit distributes gifts to each person as he sees fit. Almost everyone would say that not all Christians have the gift to perform miracles. I don't know anyone who would say that all of us have the gift of prophesy. So why would we say that all Christians should speak in tongues? We shouldn't! Just as the human body has different members with different purposes, so then the body of Christ has different members with different gifts; and the 11th verse of 1st Corinthians 12 supports this fact.

Now since this passage is clear concerning the gift of tongues, are there any other type of tongues in the Holy Bible that would indicate that all Christians are suppose to have as evidence of the Holy Spirit? The answer frankly is NO!

Let us now study the instructions concerning speaking in tongues that are given in the first book of Corinthians.

1 Corinthians 14:1-3

Follow after charity, and desire spiritual gifts, but rather that ye may prophesy. 2 For he that speaketh in an unknown tongue speaketh not unto men, but unto God: for no

---

275*Holy Bible, New Living Translation*, (Wheaton, IL: Tyndale House Publishers, Inc.) 1996.

man understandeth him; howbeit in the spirit he speaketh mysteries. 3 But he that prophesieth speaketh unto men to edification, and exhortation, and comfort. 276

Now the first thing we learn here is that an importance is placed on prophesies over tongues. The point being that we should not place an emphasis on tongues if the Holy Bible does not! Secondly, notice that verse two says, "For he that speaketh" as opposed to saying, "When we speaketh". The significance here is that this passage is not referring to every Christian, but to those Christians who have the gift of tongues. The 12th chapter of 1st Corinthians also supports the view that we all do not have the gift of tongues:

1 Corinthians 12:28-31

28 Here is a list of some of the members that God has placed in the body of Christ: first are apostles, second are prophets, third are teachers, then those who do miracles, those who have the gift of healing, those who can help others, those who can get others to work toghether, those who speak in unknown languages. 29 Is everyone an apostle? Of course not. Is everyone a prophet? No. Are all teachers? Does everyone have the power to do miracles? 30 Does everyone have the gift of healing? Of course not. Does God give all of us the ability to speak in unknown languages? Can everyone interpret unknown languages? No! 31 And in any event, you should desire the most helpful gifts. First, however, let me tell you about something else that is better than any of them! 277

276*The King James Version*, (Cambridge: Cambridge) 1769.
277*Holy Bible, New Living Translation*, (Wheaton, IL: Tyndale House Publishers, Inc.) 1996.

Let us now address a point I discussed earlier in the book. It is the point that some Christians insist on saying that speaking in tongues is the evidence of having the Holy Spirit.

The Holy Spirit produces two things, fruit of the Spirit and the gifts of the Spirit. Whatever the Holy Spirit is doing in us has to fall into one of these two categories.

Galatians 5:22-23

22 But the fruit of the Spirit is love, joy, peace, longsuffering, gentleness, goodness, faith, 23 Meekness, temperance: against such there is no law. 278

Now since there is no mention of tongues in the fruit of the Spirit category, then they have to be part of the gifts of the Spirit, and there is nowhere in the Holy Bible that indicates that every believer must have the same gift. It actually says the opposite.

Speaking in tongues is a divisive issue and probably always will be. It was a divisive issue in Paul's time, and it still is now. Paul clearly recognized speaking in tongues as an issue when he wrote to the Corinthians to give them instructions on the use of the gift.

1 Corinthians 13:1

Though I speak with the tongues of men and of angels, and have not charity, I am become as sounding brass, or a tinkling cymbal. 279

Paul here says to the Corinthians, the gift of speaking in tongues is useless if we do not have the fruit of love.

278*The King James Version*, (Cambridge: Cambridge) 1769.
279*The King James Version*, (Cambridge: Cambridge) 1769.

1 Corinthians 14:27-28

27 If any man speak in an unknown tongue, let it be by two, or at the most by three, and that by course; and let one interpret. 28 But if there be no interpreter, let him keep silence in the church; and let him speak to himself, and to God. 280

Summarizing Speaking in Tongues

First, the passages in the book of Acts that deal with speaking in tongues are not instructional but historical. We should not look to these passages as direction for us concerning tongues.

Second, the passages in the first book of Corinthians are instructional, and should be our guide concerning speaking in tongues.

Third, speaking in tongues is not a fruit but a gift according Galatians 5:22 and 1st Corinthians the 12th and 14th chapters. Since tongues are not a fruit, they should not be looked upon as evidence.

Fourth, the gift of speaking in tongues is of less importance than the fruit of love.

Fifth, the gift of tongues should not be looked upon as a necessary sign of the baptism of the Holy Spirit. We may be filled and never speak in tongues, and we may speak in tongues, and not be filled.

280*The King James Version*, (Cambridge: Cambridge) 1769.

The Rest of the Story

Although I have titled this book "The Complete Guide to Understanding the Holy Spirit", by no means do I think it is the final authority on the Holy Spirit. Neither do I personally claim to be an expert on the Holy Spirit. I simply claim that I have done an exhaustive study of this subject, as the Holy Bible tells us to do, and have documented my study in this book. It is my belief that this book helps the Christian and non-Christian with real answers to the tough questions they may have concerning the Holy Spirit.

2 Timothy 2:15

15 Study to shew thyself approved unto God, a workman that needeth not to be ashamed, rightly dividing the word of truth. 281

1 Peter 3:15

15 But sanctify the Lord God in your hearts: and be ready always to give an answer to every man that asketh you a reason of the hope that is in you with meekness and fear: 282

Various books and commentaries written by well-respected authors and theologians, unless otherwise stated, support the points that I've made in this book. They include the "KJV Bible Commentary" by Edward E. Hindson, Th.D., D.Min., and Woodrow Michael Kroll, Th.D. 283, the "Thru

---

281*The King James Version*, (Cambridge: Cambridge) 1769.
282*The King James Version*, (Cambridge: Cambridge) 1769.
283Jerry Falwell, executive editor; Edward E. Hinson and Michael Kroll Woodrow, general editors, *KJV Bible*

the Bible Commentary" by J. Vernon McGee 284, the "Holy Spirit" by Billy Graham[285], The Holy Spirt: Secret of Soul Control by June Hunt [286], and the "Matthew Henry's Commentary on the Holy Bible" 287. But more importantly, the Holy Bible supports my points.

The final authority on the Holy Spirit is the Word of God. So the rest of the story can only come from him. I invite you to study the Word of God yourself to learn who the Holy Spirit truly is, what his purpose is, and how he intended for us to use his fruit and gifts. Simply use this book as a reference, along with other great books on this subject, as you study. If you do that, I'm confident that you will come to the same conclusions that I have in the book.

commentary [computer file], electronic ed., Logos Library System, (Nashville: Thomas Nelson) 1997, c1994.
284J. Vernon McGee, *Thru the Bible commentary [computer file], electronic ed., Logos Library System,* (Nashville: Thomas Nelson) 1997, c1981 by J. Vernon McGee.
[285] The Holy Spirit by Billy Graham
[286] The Holy Spirit: Secret of Soul Control by June Hunt
287Henry, Matthew, *Matthew Henry's Commentary on the Bible,* (Peabody, MA: Hendrickson Publishers) 1997.

Resources

For information on
Tapes and other books by Wil Nichols

Contact
More Than Conquerors Publishing
Or
Victorious Praise Fellowship COGIC
P.O. Box 14392
Research Triangle Park, North Carolina 27709

Phone Toll Free: (877) 333-3VPF
(877) 333-3873

http://www.VictoriousPraise.org